LYRICS TO LIVE BY
The Beatles

LYRICS TO LIVE BY
The Beatles

A WORDS-AND-MUSIC HISTORY
of Life Lessons from Songs by John, Paul, George, and Ringo

STELLA BARNES

CASTLE POINT
PUBLISHING

This book is not authorized or sponsored by Sony Music Publishing, Sir Paul McCartney, or any other person or entity owning or controlling rights in The Beatles' name, trademarks, or copyrights.

Lyrics to Live By: The Beatles.
Copyright © 2024 by Castle Point Publishing.
Printed in China.

www.castlepointpublishing.com

All rights reserved. No portion of this book
may be reproduced or transmitted in any form
or by any means, electronic or mechanical,
including photocopying, recording, and other
information storage and retrieval systems,
without prior written permission of the publisher.

 ISBN 978-0-9988053-1-3 (paper over board)

Design by Tara Long
Editorial by Jennifer Calvert
Images used under license by Shutterstock.com

First Edition: 2024

10 9 8 7 6 5 4 3 2 1

CONTENTS

INTRODUCTION 7

LIFE 9

LOVE 37

LOSS 65

MUSIC 91

HOPE 117

SOURCES 144

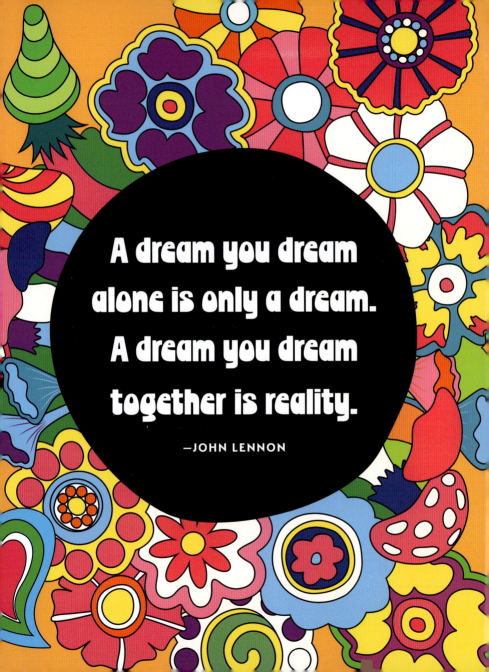

A ROCK REVOLUTION

WHETHER YOU WERE A TEEN SCRAMBLING TO BUY THEIR EPS DURING BEATLEMANIA, or you heard your first song long after the band broke up, you couldn't help but feel the incredible effect of the Beatles. Few artists have had their extraordinary worldwide musical and cultural impact. They didn't just revolutionize popular music—for more than six decades, their distinctive sound, familiar iconography, and profound social influence have all lived on alongside their incredible songs and performances.

John Lennon, Paul McCartney, Ringo Starr, and George Harrison lived a lot of life in the eight years they made music together. At the same time, the world around them was spinning quickly in a new direction. That impacted not only the evolution of their sound but also their songwriting. Hits like "Hey Jude," "Here Comes the Sun," and "Let It Be" were the stories of their lives. With fascinating trivia and personal insight from the musical icons themselves, *Lyrics to Live By: The Beatles* explores more than sixty of those stories and the things they reveal about life, love, loss, music, and hope.

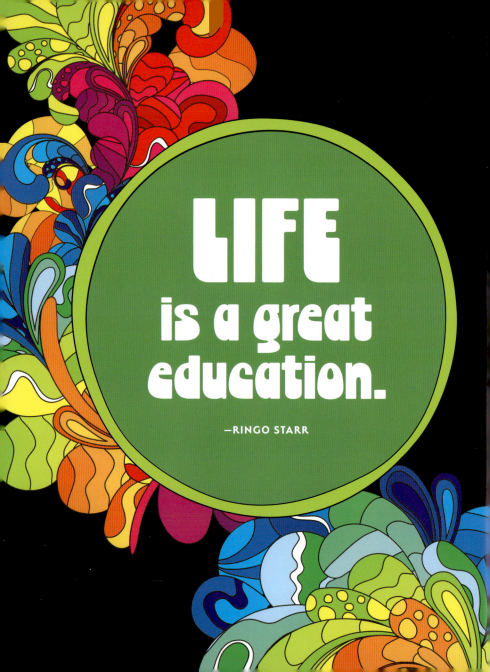

THE FAB FOUR went from being four mop-topped kids with a dream to becoming one of the most influential bands of all time in just eight years. And as their music evolved, so did they. They learned to shed expectations, embrace their experiences, express their emotions, and play to each other's strengths. From "Strawberry Fields Forever" to "Dear Prudence" and "Come Together," the songs in this section offer an inside look at that journey.

"Nowhere Man" **10**
"Strawberry Fields Forever" **13**
"Penny Lane" **14**
"Taxman" **17**
"I'm Only Sleeping" **18**
"Hello Goodbye" **21**
"Sgt. Pepper's Lonely Hearts Club Band" **22**

"Revolution" **25**
"Dear Prudence" **26**
"Across the Universe" **29**
"I'm So Tired" **30**
"Lady Madonna" **33**
"Come Together" **34**

"Nowhere Man"
RECORDED IN 1965

"Inspiration strikes when you least expect it" may as well have been the Beatles' motto. From their off-the-cuff style of writing to their wildly experimental approach to accompaniment, they seemed to embrace each moment. That doesn't mean they didn't suffer for the work at times. "Nowhere Man" is the product of both approaches—the struggle and the flow.

Whether John wrote the song about himself or about Paul has been a subject of debate over the years. For his part, Paul believed that the lyrics reflected John's frustration with his marriage to his first wife, Cynthia. With a relationship on the rocks, the pressure of worldwide fame, and a struggle with substance-abuse issues, it's not a leap to think John might have felt powerless. But at the heart of "Nowhere Man" is a reassuring message: You have more power than you think you do.

That this song came to John complete when he finally allowed himself a moment of rest is proof of that intrinsic potential. He told *Rolling Stone*, "I remember I was just going through this paranoia trying to write something and nothing would come out, so I just lay down and tried not to write . . . and then this came out." Finally letting go of the struggle and letting inspiration flow freely seemed to do the trick.

> **ON ANOTHER NOTE**
> The Beatles were constantly pushing boundaries with their music. In "Nowhere Man," Paul had the engineers use three times the allowed value of treble to get the high-pitched guitar sound he wanted.

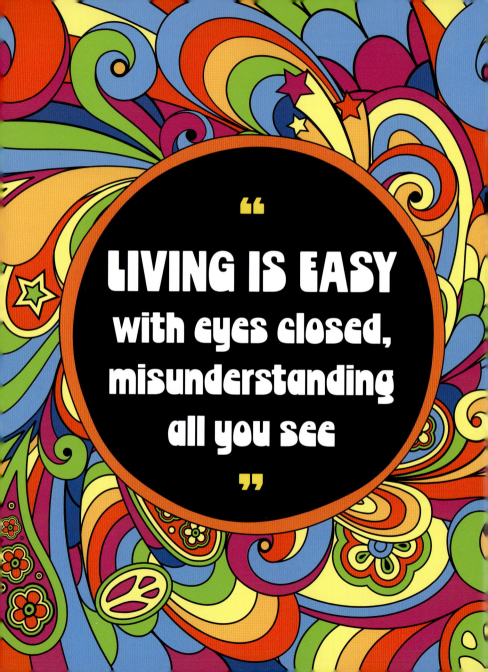

"Strawberry Fields Forever"

RECORDED IN 1966

After the Beatles retired from performing in 1966, John found himself far from home with time on his hands, and his thoughts turned to his childhood in Liverpool. But he wasn't feeling nostalgic for friends and family, or for those early days gone by. Instead, John was focused on the loneliness that had shadowed him all his life.

The unique vision John expressed throughout his career wasn't specific to his music—he had always seen the world differently. Clearly articulated in "Strawberry Fields Forever" is the feeling he says gave him a chip on his shoulder, the feeling that he knew things others couldn't understand. He told *Playboy* in a 1980 interview, "The second verse goes, 'No one I think is in my tree.' Well, I was too shy and self-doubting. Nobody seems to be as hip as me is what I was saying."

John found solace in other artists who suffered for their visions, from Oscar Wilde and Dylan Thomas to Lewis Carroll (whose influence is felt in many Beatles songs). But the desire to belong is both human and relentless. "Part of me would like to be accepted by all facets of society and not be this loudmouthed lunatic musician," he said. "But I cannot be what I am not."

> **ON ANOTHER NOTE**
> John named "Strawberry Fields Forever" after a Liverpool children's home called Strawberry Field. Although he told *Playboy* that he simply used the name as an image, the memories of playing there as a child clearly inspired the song's subject as well.

"Penny Lane"
RECORDED IN 1966

Healthy competition can be a productive force when properly applied. In many cases, John and Paul found themselves spurred on by the best musicians of their time to create something better, smarter, catchier, and more innovative. And when they weren't focused on outdoing their fellow performers, the bandmates were quite happy to compete with each other.

"Penny Lane" was a product of that competitive streak. Named for a street and its surrounding area in Paul and John's childhood hometown, the song was Paul's nostalgia-filled answer to John's "Strawberry Fields Forever." Their good-natured rivalry paid off with an iconic hit that put the small neighborhood on the map. Penny Lane became so popular with fans that it had to replace its frequently stolen street signs with painted ones.

The song paints the picture of a quaint suburban hamlet filled with friendly people (and a few mischievous children). The cheerful nature of the music complements the song's idyllic setting, but its composition is far more complex than many realize. Recording it took nine takes of layering in vocals, harmonies, multiple pianos, guitars, drums and congas, a tambourine, and an arrangement of brass and wind instruments. And after all was said and done, Paul recruited a trumpet player he'd seen on the BBC to complete the piece.

> **ON ANOTHER NOTE**
> "Penny Lane" and "Strawberry Fields Forever" were meant to be central to the *Sgt. Pepper* album but were released as singles under pressure from the label. Producer George Martin called taking the songs off the album "the biggest mistake of [his] career."

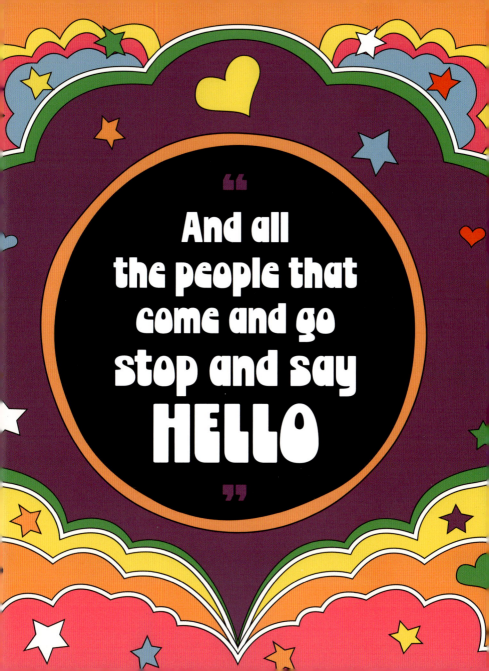

"Taxman"

RECORDED IN 1966

They say only two things are certain in life: death and taxes. George Harrison channeled his frustration with the latter into a resentful rock song that would resonate with fans for decades. He called "Taxman" his most autobiographical Beatles song.

The Beatles' rise to international fame was no small feat—it was the result of its members' blood, sweat, and calloused fingers. The band spent an extraordinary 300 studio hours producing *Revolver* alone (the album on which "Taxman" appears). When the Beatles started to feel the financial success of their efforts, George realized the British government was levying an incredibly hefty 90 percent tax on their earnings. With a rousing beat and the power of electric guitar, he issued a resounding personal protest.

This anti-establishment anthem named names for the first time in Beatles history. By calling out Mr. Harold Wilson, the newly elected Labour Party prime minister, and Mr. Edward Heath, the leader of the Conservative Party, its lyrics come down on both political parties. The song's message of frustration remains just as relevant across governments today.

> **ON ANOTHER NOTE**
> The Lennon–McCartney writing partnership was well established early on in Beatles history. By playing off each other's strengths and imagination, the duo created music magic. And they knew it. When George asked for input on his songs, neither man wanted to volunteer. John told *Playboy* his initial response to collaborating on "Taxman" was, "Oh, no, don't tell me I have to work on George's stuff." But in the end, he "bit [his] tongue and said OK."

"I'm Only Sleeping"
RECORDED IN 1966

Given that so many Beatles songs were influenced and even inspired by the band's affection for mind-altering substances, it's little wonder that fans assume "I'm Only Sleeping" is one of them. But the truth is, John simply loved to sleep. Journalist Maureen Cleave called him "probably the laziest person in England," to which he responded, "Physically lazy. I don't mind writing or reading or watching or speaking."

John began writing the brilliant defense of his napping habit after noticing Paul's tendency to wake him for work in the afternoon. Together, they completed the song in one session. Recording it, however, was far more laborious, thanks to the Beatles' perpetual quest to create new and exciting sounds. Speed changes and a reverse guitar solo gave the song the hazy, slowly awakening aura they were hoping for.

Paul has said that the song is about the luxury of being able to sleep, meditate, and lie around. And in a world that seems to spin more quickly every day, it certainly is a luxury. But the song also cautions that resting isn't lazy—it's essential to creativity, productivity, and sanity.

> **ON ANOTHER NOTE**
> After hearing the tape mistakenly played backward, Paul exclaimed, "My God, that's fantastic! Can we do that for real?" George Harrison and producer George Martin then spent several painstaking hours recording the reversed arrangement beat by beat. The result is a trippy, yawning effect that completes this dreamy composition.

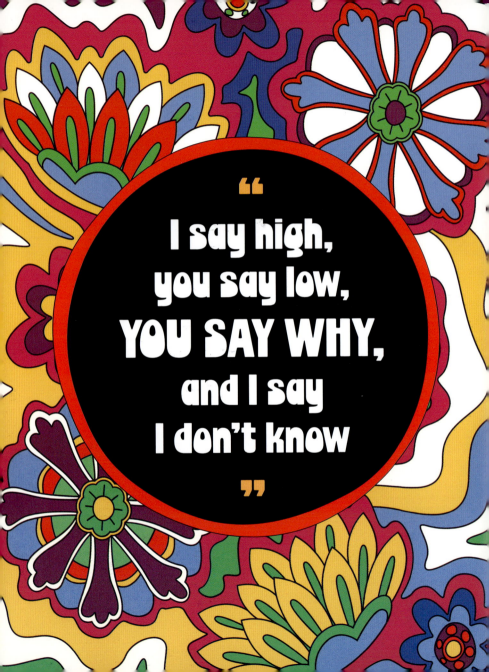

"Hello Goodbye"
RECORDED IN 1967

One of the many things that made the Beatles the transformational musicians they were was their ability to find cohesion in contrasting elements. From lyrics to arrangements, they always created balance. And so much of that is due to the songwriting duo of Lennon and McCartney. Throughout their friendship and collaboration, Paul had always been the bright, positive yang to John's dark and moody yin.

"Hello Goodbye" is a distillation of Paul. He still considers himself "the eternal optimist" and asserts that "No matter how rough it gets, there's always light somewhere." That tendency toward cheerfulness and hope sometimes irked John, but it also steadied him. And it helped keep the Beatles at the top of the charts. When they released "Hello Goodbye" as a single, they did so opposite John's "I Am the Walrus." The former, which was clearly the more commercially viable of the two, was No. 1 in the US for three weeks and in the UK for seven.

The song began as lightly as its lyrics. Paul was simply giving a songwriting lesson to assistant Alistair Taylor and said, "Whenever I shout out a word, you shout the opposite, and I'll make up a tune." But years later, Paul saw it as more of a philosophical commentary: "It's such a deep theme in the universe, duality."

> **ON ANOTHER NOTE**
> John remained irked by the success of "Hello Goodbye" for decades, particularly because it was chosen as the A-side of the single over "I Am the Walrus." He considered his song the superior of the two.

"Sgt. Pepper's Lonely Hearts Club Band"
RECORDED IN 1967

Compared to other iconic musical groups, the Beatles lasted only a short time. (The Rolling Stones, for example, have been active for six decades.) But in their all-too-brief eight years, the Beatles were constantly reinventing both themselves and the music industry. Coupled with international fame and success, that reputation for innovation resulted in the sometimes-crushing pressure to produce the next big thing.

In 1966, Paul had an idea to combat the stress of those rising expectations: an entire album created from the perspective of someone else. As Paul put it, "Everything about the album will be imagined from the perspective of these people, so it doesn't have to be the kind of song you want to write, it could be the song they might want to write." Paul meant for *Sgt. Pepper* to be that album, and for the title song to introduce the premise.

> **ON ANOTHER NOTE**
> The fictional Sgt. Pepper got his name from a simple misunderstanding over a shared airplane dinner. Paul misheard roadie Mal Evans when he mumbled "salt and pepper" and immediately saw Sgt. Pepper as a character.

The band ended up writing only two of the album's songs from this perspective—the title song (and, therefore, its reprise) and "With a Little Help from My Friends." But by stepping into the shoes of this other group, the Fab Four were free to release even their own creative constraints for a few moments. "Sgt. Pepper's Lonely Hearts Club Band" is more proof from the Beatles that letting go can lead to great things.

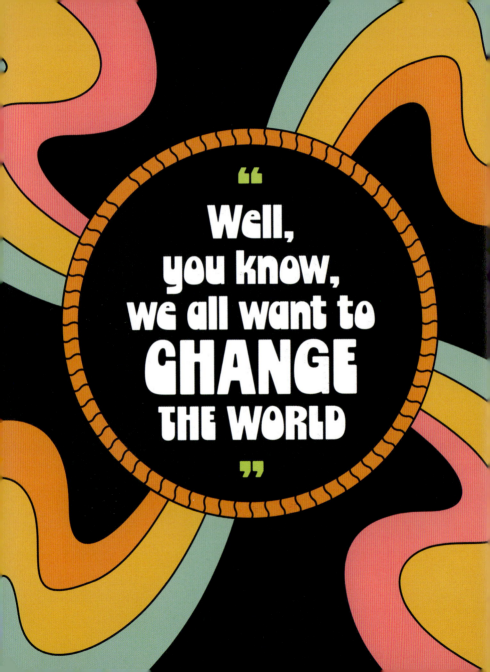

"Revolution"
RECORDED IN 1968

There came a point during the political turmoil of the 1960s that the Beatles decided they couldn't shy away from expressing their personal opinions anymore. As the band drew their creative inspiration from the world around them, songs like "Revolution" and "Blackbird" were a natural extension of that decision. With the former, John wanted the world to know where he stood. But the number itself would go through a few revolutions before becoming the one fans readily recognize today.

The first version of the song, now referred to as "Revolution 1," was slower, had a decidedly bluesy bent, and featured one word that changed everything: "in." It went, "When you talk about destruction / Don't you know that you can count me out . . . in." (Paul referred to this as John "hedging his bets.") Since the other three Beatles weren't thrilled with the song's plodding tempo, John reluctantly agreed to a more upbeat arrangement. And by the time they recorded the single, the word "in" had disappeared.

Still, "Revolution" was just the beginning of the band members' political engagement. In 1980, John told *Playboy*, "The lyrics stand today. It's still my feeling about politics." But the years seemed to have softened his stance on revolution, as he followed that statement by saying conclusively, "Count me out if it is for violence."

> If someone thinks that peace and love are just a cliché that must have been left behind in the '60s, that's a problem. Peace and love are eternal.
> —JOHN LENNON

"Dear Prudence"
RECORDED IN 1968

If there was one thing the Beatles had learned by 1968, it was that fame comes at a cost—to privacy, personal freedom, relaxation, and connection. The more mired you become in trying to achieve it, the more you can lose your sense of self. In *The Beatles Anthology*, Paul revealed that the band came to share a feeling of "Yeah, well, it's great to be famous, it's great to be rich—but what's it all for?" They sought their answer in Rishikesh, India.

After following the work of Transcendental Meditation guru Maharishi Mahesh Yogi for some time, the four band members and their significant others made a trip to study under him at his ashram. George and John, in particular, found solace in the retreat's seclusion and daily meditation. With their creative batteries finally able to recharge, the Beatles wrote dozens of songs there.

One of those numbers, "Dear Prudence," was inspired by a fellow seeker who happened to be actress Mia Farrow's younger sister. Prudence Farrow barely left her room, choosing instead to fully immerse herself in meditation. (Prudence eventually became a Transcendental Meditation teacher herself.) The soft, guitar-led song was John's way of coaxing her out to see the beauty that surrounded them in the foothills of the Himalayas.

> **ON ANOTHER NOTE**
> At the time the Beatles recorded "Dear Prudence," Ringo had briefly quit the band due to rising tensions among its members. Luckily, all of the Beatles were multitalented musicians. Paul played the drums—as well as bass, piano, and flugelhorn—for the song.

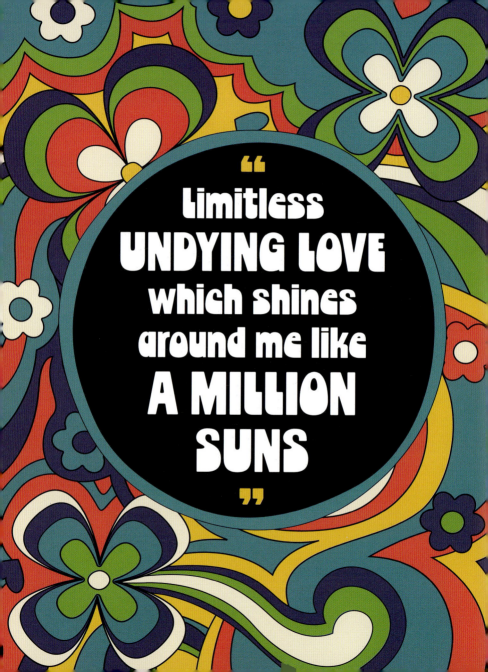

"Across the Universe"
RECORDED IN 1969

Part of the skill of songwriting is recognizing inspiration when it strikes, and that's something that the Beatles were particularly adept at. John told journalist David Sheff that he didn't own "Across the Universe" because the song came to him fully formed. He was stewing about a fight with his first wife, Cynthia, when its words seemed to permeate his thoughts. He simply wrote them down.

John later told *Rolling Stone*, "It's one of the best lyrics I've written. In fact, it could be the best." Meeting inspiration, it turned out, was more difficult than recognizing it. Although he was pleased with his work, he felt the band never did the song justice. In Sheff's *Playboy* interview, John accused Paul of subconsciously sabotaging his "great songs" by experimenting with them rather than refining them.

In truth, the band and engineers tried instrument after instrument, vocal after vocal, but none matched the music that John heard in his head. Finally, John gave up and offered the song to Britain's World Wildlife Fund for a charity album. But when producer Phil Spector reworked the song for the *Let It Be* album with an orchestra and choir, John said he "did a damn good job with it."

> **ON ANOTHER NOTE**
> With a Sanskrit mantra in the refrain, it's clear that "Across the Universe" was partially inspired by John's interest in Maharishi Mahesh Yogi. In fact, the phrase "Jai guru deva om" is a saying of the Maharishi's teacher Guru Dev, meaning "Victory to God Divine."

"I'm So Tired"
RECORDED IN 1968

Years of feeling stuck in an unhappy marriage left John numbing his pain in a number of ways. But when he and the others went to India to study with Maharishi Mahesh Yogi, he found himself face-to-face with his problems without any of his usual crutches—the Maharishi forbade them. They were replaced by a combination of meditation and insomnia that left John hallucinating and exhausted.

With John's well-documented affection for rest, it's easy to understand the increasing desperation he conveys in "I'm So Tired." John's tiredness wasn't just physical, it was also existential. His discontent had reached a tipping point. In the lyrics, he curses Sir Walter Raleigh (the explorer credited with bringing tobacco to England), but it was really Yoko Ono who was haunting his thoughts.

> **ON ANOTHER NOTE**
> Ringo and his wife, Maureen, also felt uneasy at the ashram, but for entirely different reasons. "You'd have to fight off the scorpions and tarantulas in a bath," he said in *The Beatles Anthology*. They left after just ten days.

John had become infatuated with Yoko, going so far as to consider bringing both her and his wife on the trip. He eagerly left Cynthia each morning to see if he'd received a letter from Yoko that day. The peace of mind he's pleading for in "I'm So Tired" could only come with the end of his first marriage. With that in mind, the song becomes a stark lesson in resolving your problems so they don't leave you tossing and turning at night.

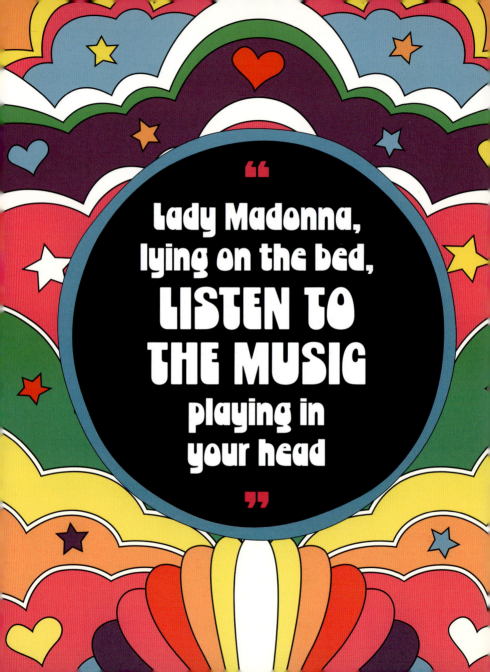

"Lady Madonna"
RECORDED IN 1968

Paul began writing "Lady Madonna" with the Virgin Mary in mind, but his vision quickly extended to include the many Catholic working-class women he'd met in Liverpool. Later, he would say that his inspiration came from a photo in *National Geographic* of a mother breastfeeding one child while another looked up at her, laughing. The photograph, which appeared in the January 1965 issue, was titled "Mountain Madonna." He looked at it and was struck by the mother's strength.

In championing Lady Madonna's maternal determination and resilience, Paul hints at a personal philosophy of his own: the power of music to fortify a person. One of the reasons that the Beatles continued to evolve and create great music was their willingness to be moved by the music of others. Rather than being envious or resentful of the talents of their fellow musicians, the Beatles constantly looked for what they could learn from them.

In this case, Paul was looking to American artist Fats Domino and his uniquely New Orleans sound. He completed the homage by adding tenor saxophones to his bluesy piano lick. Domino repaid the compliment just a few months later by releasing a cover version of the song. It was his last Hot 100 hit.

> **ON ANOTHER NOTE**
> John was never impressed with "Lady Madonna," telling David Sheff that "the song never really went anywhere." In fact, it went to the top of the charts in both the UK and US, peaking at No. 2 and 4, respectively.

"Come Together"
RECORDED IN 1969

When John began writing "Come Together," it was as a favor to California gubernatorial candidate (and LSD proponent) Timothy Leary, whose slogan was "Come together, join the party." But Leary's campaign against Ronald Reagan ended abruptly when he was jailed for possession of marijuana, freeing John from his commitment. The finished song is far from the "chant-along thing" John wrote for his friend.

Fans who can't make heads or tails of its lyrics aren't missing anything—the words are a mixture of gibberish and inside jokes. The only truly discernable soundbite is John's plea for freedom at the heart of it. But the important takeaway from "Come Together" is how it really did bring the Beatles together at a time when they were beginning to fall apart. Each member had a hand in writing the song, and each contributed his unique talents to its arrangement.

> The Beatles were just four guys that loved each other. That's all they'll ever be.
> —RINGO STARR

"Come Together" was like a last hurrah for the Beatles, a testament to the magic of their collaboration. Producer George Martin remembered it fondly, saying, "If I had to pick one song that showed the four disparate talents of the boys and the ways they combined to make a great sound, I would choose 'Come Together. . . .' The four of them became much, much better than the individual components." Even John called it one of his favorite Beatles tracks. But this rallying song would be the last they cut together before John left in search of freedom.

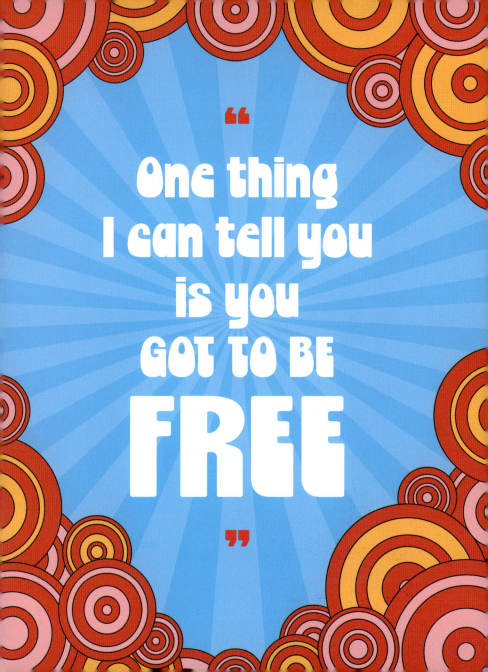

FROM SINGING ABOUT LOVE to preaching love and practicing love (in all its forms), this is the subject the Beatles may be most associated with. But their sweetest love songs were just as often born from lusting after their next hit as they were from swooning over partners. In appealing to the love of their fans, though, they forged their relationships with each other. And, through the songs in this section, the Beatles demonstrated their love for each other and for their music.

"Please Please Me" **39**
"Love Me Do" **40**
"I Want to Hold Your Hand" **43**
"She Loves You" **44**
"All My Loving" **47**
"A Hard Day's Night" **48**
"If I Fell" **51**

"We Can Work It Out" **52**
"Here, There and Everywhere" **55**
"All You Need Is Love" **56**
"Don't Let Me Down" **59**
"The Ballad of John and Yoko" **60**
"Two of Us" **63**

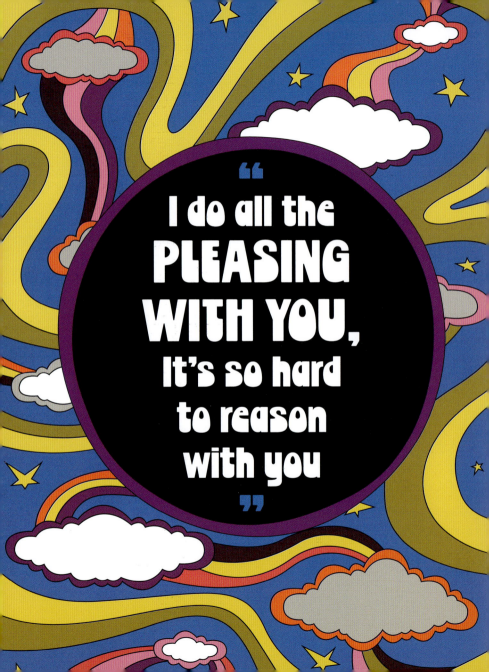

"Please Please Me"
RECORDED IN 1962

The lyrics of "Please Please Me" seem like the pleading of a lovelorn songwriter, but love was the last thing on John's mind when writing it. As usual, he was focused on the music—Roy Orbison's music, to be exact. "Only the Lonely" was No. 1 in Britain, inspiring John to try his hand at its slow style and clever word play.

Although the resulting song lamented mismatched efforts in love, its creation forged the relationship between the fresh-faced Beatles and their new producer, George Martin. With only the simple "Love Me Do" and "P.S. I Love You" to their credit, Martin wasn't all that optimistic about the Beatles' original work. But in life as in the song, you must be willing to meet in the middle. He suggested that a change in tempo might do "Please Please Me" some good. It changed everything.

"We lifted the tempo, and suddenly there was that fast Beatles spirit," Paul later recounted. Not only did the Fab Four find their stride, they also proved to Martin that they had what it took to make it big. At the end of the recording session, he said, "Gentlemen, I think you've got your first No. 1." In fact, it was the first of four consecutive No. 1 hits and the beginning of Beatlemania in Britain.

> **ON ANOTHER NOTE**
> John's Aunt Mimi, with whom he was living at the time, wasn't a fan of the band's first single, "Love Me Do." When she heard "Please Please Me," she told John, "That's more like it. That should do well."

"Love Me Do"
RECORDED IN 1962

The A-side of the Beatles' first single, "Love Me Do," sounds like more of an appeal to listeners than to any real-life person. And, of course, listeners happily obliged. But John and Paul wrote the song years before their words and mop tops inspired hysteria among crowds of thousands of young women. In 1958, they were just teenagers in Liverpool dreaming of such a scene.

The simple, straightforward song made it to No. 17 on the UK charts (helped along by manager Brian Epstein buying 10,000 copies for his own store), proving the wisdom of pursuing one's dreams. But "Love Me Do" didn't fill producer George Martin with affection for the band. His first impression of the Lennon–McCartney partnership was that "their songwriting was crap." He wondered, "Oh, God, where am I going to get a good song for them?"

But Martin would discover he had a knack for bringing out the Beatles' best. He suggested adding a harmonica to the arrangement, and it just so happened that John was prepared for such an occasion. Paul took over lead vocals (for the first time), and the rest was music history.

ON ANOTHER NOTE
After recording "Please Please Me" that same day, George Martin benched Ringo and replaced him with a session drummer for "Love Me Do." Ringo later said it was because "while we were recording ['Please Please Me'], I was playing a bass drum with a maraca in one hand and a tambourine in the other." But Ringo quickly proved his skills and earned an apology from Martin.

"I Want to Hold Your Hand"

RECORDED IN 1963

In the somber days that followed the assassination of President John F. Kennedy, no one could have guessed that a cheerful tune from a group of British musicians would send shockwaves through the United States. But "I Want to Hold Your Hand" changed everything, for American music and for the Fab Four themselves. The sweet, forthright song with its rousing sound brought Beatlemania stateside.

Like the feelings building between the lovers in the song, the Beatles' fame was beginning to bubble up and over by 1963. Then, when an American teenage girl begged a Washington, D.C., DJ to play their newest hit, they were catapulted to the top of the US charts. With a No. 1 record under their belt, the Beatles made their first trip across the pond to appear on *The Ed Sullivan Show* in front of a record-breaking 70 million viewers.

> **ON ANOTHER NOTE**
> Demand for "I Want to Hold Your Hand" exploded after its first play, which inspired a reluctant Capitol Records not only to produce the single but also to fast-track it. The song sold more than 1 million copies in its first few weeks.

"I Want to Hold Your Hand" was more than just a lively love song inspired by Paul's girlfriend, Jane Asher. It was also a product of the fresh-faced optimism and comradery that filled the band's early days. Paul and John wrote the song side by side at Jane's family's piano, their voices expertly playing off one another's. In life as in the lyrics, that enthusiasm was enthralling.

"She Loves You"
RECORDED IN 1963

The story of "She Loves You" begins, simply enough, with Bobby Rydell's "Forget Him" inspiring Paul to write a song in the third person. As usual, John and Paul found themselves playing off each other's ideas, acoustic guitars in hand. This time, they happened to do it from opposite twin beds in the Turks Hotel in Newcastle-upon-Tyne. They finished the song the next day, back at Paul's home in Liverpool. Nothing in the normalcy of their songwriting process could have prepared them for what came next.

On July 1, 1963, a crowd gathered to watch the Beatles take photos in the alleyway behind their studio. By the time the band began recording "She Loves You," that crowd had overwhelmed police and stormed, screaming, into the studio. Rather than be alarmed by the chaos, the musicians were energized by it. The resulting adrenaline rush helped them create Great Britain's best-selling single of the decade.

"She Loves You" is largely recognized as a tipping point in the Beatles' exceptional career. From its collaborative creation to its remarkable recording and its wildly popular reception, this lively pop song has come to symbolize the epitome of Beatlemania. With an unassuming song written from a new perspective, the Beatles learned that a small shift can change everything.

> **ON ANOTHER NOTE**
> Upon hearing the song, Paul's father lamented the Americanization of British culture and asked his son if he could change the now-iconic "yeah, yeah, yeah" to a more proper "yes, yes, yes." Thankfully, Paul responded, "You don't understand, Dad. It wouldn't work."

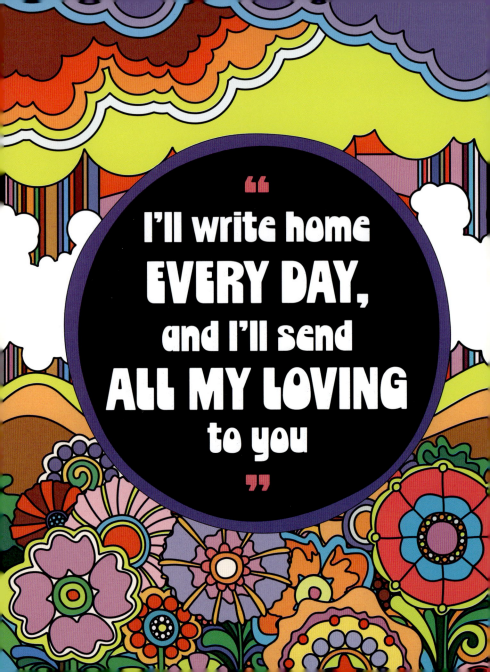

"All My Loving"
RECORDED IN 1963

While touring with Roy Orbison, Paul set out to write a song with a bit of an American-country flavor. (George was particularly happy to work in the genre. He was such a fan of rockabilly pioneer Carl Perkins that he'd used the stage name "Carl Harrison" in tribute during the Beatles' early days.) Paul didn't have to look far for the inspiration—he wrote the song on the tour bus between stops.

By this point in their career, the Beatles had grown accustomed to leaving their loved ones to go out on the road. Some have speculated that Paul had longtime girlfriend Jane Asher in mind while writing. But he wasn't as true as his lyrics promised. In proper country fashion, his unfaithfulness eventually ended their relationship.

"All My Loving" was the first of only a few songs throughout his career that Paul wrote words-first. Without a guitar handy, he wrote the accompaniment on a piano he found backstage at the band's next gig. Paul quickly realized that "All My Loving" was perfect for the Beatles' live set. They even used the song to open their first appearance on *The Ed Sullivan Show* (which, of course, also happened to be their US debut).

ON ANOTHER NOTE
John could be a harsh critic of his fellow Beatles, but he admitted to *Playboy* interviewer David Sheff in 1980 that "All My Loving" was "a damn good piece of work." Of course, he was quick to add, "But I play a pretty mean guitar in the back."

"A Hard Day's Night"
RECORDED IN 1964

As many fans know, "A Hard Day's Night" was more than a Beatles song—it was also a musical comedy starring the Fab Four themselves. The title came from an offhand comment Ringo made after a long day of recording. He said, "It's been a hard day," and then, noticing it was dark outside, quickly added ". . . 's night." It was the perfect name for a film focused on the exhilarating and exhausting aspects of Beatlemania.

As filming drew to a close on April 15, 1964, the movie still needed a title song. John came roaring in the next morning with "A Hard Day's Night," and the band had it on tape the day after that with just a three-hour recording session. Much of the production of the song took its cinematic purpose into account, with director Richard Lester putting in his two cents along the way. His insistence on a strong start led to John playing around until he struck the now-famous opening chord. And the film's need for a scene transition resulted in George's fading guitar arpeggios at the end.

Although the song is about love smoothing the rough edges of life, another message rings clear: how loving your work can make the long days and weariness worth it. Having adoring fans probably didn't hurt, though.

ON ANOTHER NOTE
A Hard Day's Night, the movie, follows the four bandmates for thirty-six hours as they navigate work, fame, and Paul's trouble-making grandfather (played by Wilfrid Brambell). It was a huge commercial success and is still considered by many to be one of the great movies of all time.

"If I Fell"
RECORDED IN 1964

Although John is most often remembered for his incredible impact on rock music, he also wrote several standout ballads for the Beatles. "If I Fell" was his first, an intimate look at a side of John he hardly seemed to know himself at the time. His lyrics emanate a vulnerability he couldn't admit to: his own fear of rejection and loneliness.

Paul later said of John, "People tend to think of him as an acerbic wit and aggressive and abrasive, but he did have a very warm side to him, really, which he didn't like to show too much in case he got rejected." With that in mind, fans can understand why John referred to "If I Fell" as semi-autobiographical despite being with his wife, Cynthia, at the time of writing it. The song was another of many manifestations of his discontent in life and in love.

At the time, that lack of trust didn't extend to John's partnership with Paul (however competitive the duo might have been). "If I Fell" illustrated the pair's natural talent for harmonizing. They even shared a microphone during recording to emphasize their unity.

> **ON ANOTHER NOTE**
> John fully embraced his softer side years later, after marrying Yoko Ono and having their son, Sean. He told David Sheff in 1980 that he was proud to be a househusband and give up his role as a "macho rock-and-roll singer." He radiated a happiness that seemed to elude him at the time of writing "If I Fell."

"We Can Work It Out"
RECORDED IN 1965

Every relationship has its struggles, but compassion, connection, and communication can help you move past them. Inflexibility, on the other hand, might create a rift that you just can't cross. That's the uneasy message Paul imparts in "We Can Work It Out," which was inspired by an argument he had with then-girlfriend Jane Asher. Paul wrote the lion's share of the lyrics while John wrote the bridge.

Although the song's music generally feels upbeat and encouraging, there's a sense of urgency about the lyrics and a hint of darkness provided by the minor-key bridge. That's because listeners find themselves in the middle of a divide not just between the song's subjects but also between its writers. John described his middle eight as "impatient" while calling Paul's lyrics "optimistic." The noticeable difference between the lines "we can work it out" and "life is very short" is characteristic of the pair's divergent philosophies. But the song ends on a hopeful note, both literally and figuratively.

> **ON ANOTHER NOTE**
> George suggested the rhythm change, which worked nicely with the sound of the old, leftover harmonium the band utilized for this song.

"We Can Work It Out" continued the band's streak of chart-topping singles in the United States. (To this day, the Beatles hold the record for most No. 1 hits, with twenty of them.) The song also topped the band's record for number of hours spent working in the studio on a single track. It took eleven hours to perfect, but the effort was well worth the result.

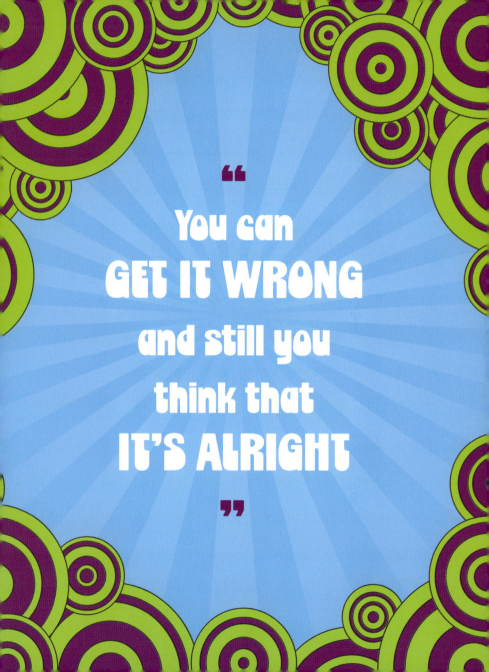

"Here, There and Everywhere"

RECORDED IN 1966

At a time when the Beatles had any number of instruments and effects at their disposal—and experimented with them freely—"Here, There and Everywhere" rang out with clarion simplicity. The music echoes the effortless love story the song tells. Its production, however, was not effortless. "Here, There and Everywhere" took three days to record, with layer upon layer added to create the song's ethereal sound.

Paul wrote the song on a sun chair by John's swimming pool, strumming on a guitar, while waiting for the famously sleepy Beatle to wake up one June morning. As was often the case, Paul found his inspiration for the lyrics in girlfriend Jane Asher and his vision for the music in other artists—this time, the Beach Boys. He had received a copy of their album *Pet Sounds* earlier in the year and was blown away by it. Brian Wilson's influence is obvious in Paul's chord sequence. Not quite as obvious is Paul's homage to Marianne Faithfull, whose voice he tried to mimic while recording the song.

"Here, There and Everywhere" wasn't just a hit with fans. John and Paul both recalled in later years the smooth, straightforward song as a favorite of theirs. It stands as proof that in love and in music, the simple things are often the best.

> One of my biggest thrills for me still is sitting down with a guitar or a piano and just out of nowhere trying to make a song happen.
> —PAUL McCARTNEY

"All You Need Is Love"
RECORDED IN 1967

They say necessity is the mother of invention. It does seem to have prodded John's imagination along more than once. One of the most quintessential of Beatles songs, "All You Need Is Love," was one of those works created out of obligation rather than inspiration. But its impact, like its message, has still stood the test of time.

The Beatles crafted the song just days before its debut on the first international satellite broadcast—a television program called *Our World*, which would connect 400 million viewers over five continents. Although they laid down some of the elements in advance, John, Paul, and George all played and sang live for the broadcast. (For technical reasons, Ringo's drumming was prerecorded.) They were joined in the studio by a thirteen-piece orchestra and the likes of Mick Jagger, Keith Richards, Marianne Faithfull, and Eric Clapton, to name a few.

The international flavor of "All You Need Is Love" was producer George Martin's contribution. He later said that the band told him, "Write absolutely anything you like, George." He chose "La Marseillaise," the French national anthem, as the lead-in and Bach's "Greensleeves" for the coda because they were both in the public domain. Just as it was meant to, the song spread the message of love and peace the world over.

> **ON ANOTHER NOTE**
> If you watch the *Our World* broadcast, you can clearly see both John and Paul chewing gum while singing. This isn't uncommon, either for the Beatles or for other musicians. Chewing gum helps keep the mouth and throat from drying out while performing.

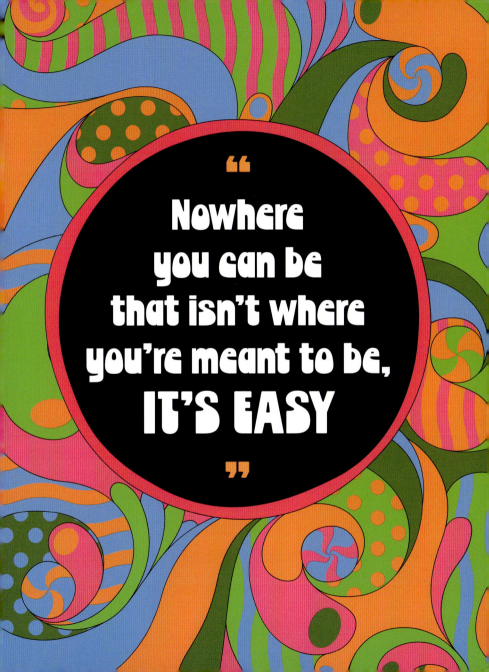

"Don't Let Me Down"
RECORDED IN 1969

Don't let the simplicity of this song's lyrics fool you. Another of John's deeply honest declarations of love for Yoko Ono, "Don't Let Me Down" is filled with desperation and passion. In just a few words, he describes a love that feels eternal, erasing everything that came before it and infusing the future with hope. But giving yourself over to another person can be as terrifying as it is exhilarating. John wanted the audience to feel what he was feeling at the time—a sense of drowning in love and calling out for the other person.

In order to achieve that intensity, John knew he'd need to start strong. He asked Ringo to lead him in with a cymbal crash, giving him "the courage to come screaming in," as he put it. The cymbals continuing in the chorus also offset the steadier, more soulful tones in the verse, creating the sense of waves slowly building and suddenly crashing.

The Beatles included the song in what would become the band's last live performance, their then-secret, now-famous rooftop concert at Apple Corps in central London on January 20, 1969. John left the band to start a new life with the woman who inspired it not long afterward. Knowing that, the song's angst-ridden plea reads as that of a man about to leap into the unknown and imploring his lover to catch him. That raw emotion still captivates fans today.

> As usual, there is a great woman behind every idiot.
> —JOHN LENNON

"The Ballad of John and Yoko"
RECORDED IN 1969

Although John said in later years that he felt Paul resented Yoko, the trio's work on "The Ballad of John and Yoko" tells another story, one of friendship, brotherhood, and love. The lyrics tell the story of John and Yoko's whirlwind wedding and honeymoon. In this upbeat folk song, John demonstrates how something that should be so easy—love—is complicated by fame and politics.

The plan was simple and romantic: get married on a cross-channel ferry. But because Yoko wasn't English, she wasn't allowed to board. Just as the song says, assistant Peter Brown offered Gibraltar as an alternative. The couple were married at the British Consulate there before staging their famous bed-in for peace at the Amsterdam Hilton Hotel. (They assumed their honeymoon would be front-page news either way, so they decided to use it for a good cause.)

John was eager to record the song upon his return, but George and Ringo were both out of town. Paul stepped up to help his friend, and the two played all the parts. The video for "The Ballad of John and Yoko" shows the couple not just on their travels but also in the studio, with Yoko sitting in while John and Paul record.

> **ON ANOTHER NOTE**
> The chorus of the song begins with "Christ!" and ends with "They're going to crucify me." When Paul read the lyrics, he warned John against them, citing the upset caused by his famous statement, "We're more popular than Jesus." The man who murdered John in 1980 said at the time he was enraged by that statement.

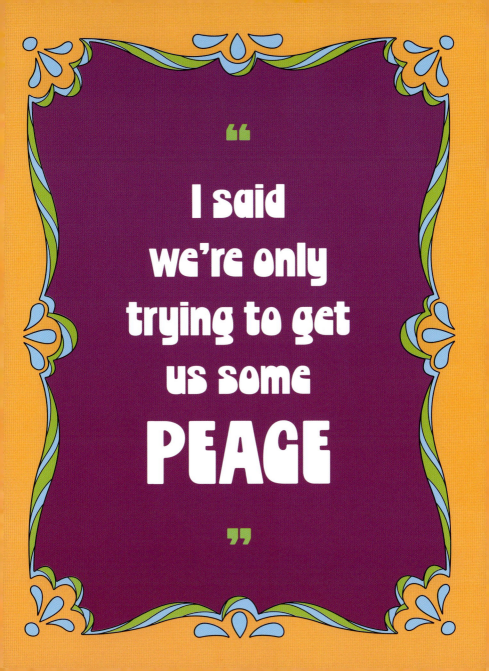

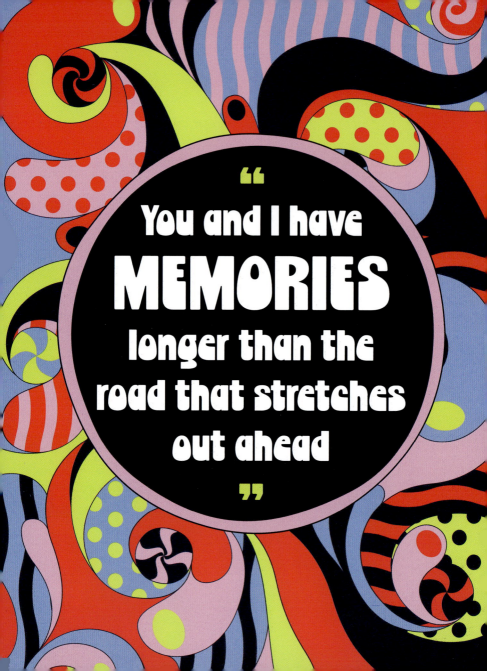

"Two of Us"

RECORDED IN 1969

At a time when nothing was simple for the Beatles, Paul was able to find joy in the simplicity of his early romance with photographer and future wife Linda Eastman. She encouraged Paul to step off the beaten path (quite literally), from getting lost on the roads of London late at night to setting out on adventures in the countryside. He wrote "Two of Us" on one such road trip, parked with his guitar in the middle of the woods while Linda went for a walk.

Between the buoyant harmonies, upbeat strumming, and calming lyrics, this sweet ballad is a bright spot on *Let It Be*. Paul's happiness is palpable. But, as is often the case, the song also works as a commentary on this time in the Beatles' career. With Yoko taking a more prominent place in John's life, it was becoming clear that he wanted to leave the band. And Paul was relieved to find refuge in Linda and their travels.

Despite the tension in the group, John and Paul stood together at the microphone to create their shining harmonies. Their relationship, with its countless vibrant memories, may have been coming to a fork in the road. But they shared an amazing ride. And with their partners by their sides, they found a new sense of home.

ON ANOTHER NOTE
Tensions were high between bandmates in the year before they ultimately dissolved the Beatles. Around the time they recorded "Two of Us," Paul and George got into an argument that led to George leaving the band. He returned just a few days later.

IN THEIR EIGHT YEARS TOGETHER, members of the Beatles were married and divorced, lost dear friends, and discovered the immense importance of trust. Their injuries ranged from shockingly sudden to agonizingly gradual. The end of the band was both. But through the pain of loss, beautifully depicted in songs like "Yesterday" and "Hey Jude," the Fab Four grew into themselves and looked toward the future.

"No Reply" **67**
"Things We Said Today" **68**
"I'm a Loser" **71**
"Yesterday" **72**
"The Night Before" **75**
"You've Got to Hide Your Love Away" **76**

"You Won't See Me" **79**
"Eleanor Rigby" **80**
"She's Leaving Home" **83**
"Hey Jude" **84**
"Get Back" **87**
"The Long and Winding Road" **88**

"No Reply"
RECORDED IN 1964

With Beatlemania in full swing and John a married father to little Julian, the Beatles were no longer starry-eyed, guitar-picking kids. John wasn't yet expressing his full life experience in his songs, but he was beginning to explore deeper themes. "No Reply" is an important lyrical line in the sand.

A shift in tone from the sweet, innocent ditties that marked the band's early days, this song explored the sadder side of young love. According to John, his inspiration for the lyrics came from the 1957 song "Silhouettes" by the Rays and not any real-life scenario. But with youth and fame, trust is hard to come by. It's well known that the Beatles struggled with infidelity.

In his 1980 *Playboy* interview, John described himself as "a very jealous, possessive guy." His first wife, Cynthia, substantiated that. In her book *John*, she wrote that John accused her of cheating, threatened a custody battle, and had her followed by a private investigator when they divorced. He, of course, had been having an affair with Yoko Ono at the time.

Considering the drama the Beatles faced in their personal lives, "No Reply" is still innocent by comparison. It just scratches the surface of heartbreak. But it allowed the band to break through with more meaningful and expressive songs down the line.

> **ON ANOTHER NOTE**
> John and Paul wrote many songs for other artists under their Lennon–McCartney songwriting partnership. "No Reply" was originally meant for Tommy Quickly, another musician under Brian Epstein's management. He decided not to use the song, so the Beatles recorded it themselves.

"Things We Said Today"
RECORDED IN 1964

Successful, in love, and yachting in the Virgin Islands, Paul couldn't have been in a better place to write "Things We Said Today." Its sentiment stands as sage advice for any relationship: hold on to the memories of being together whenever you're apart, and look back on them fondly when you're older. But the minor key gives the song a dark edge that stands in opposition to its sunny outlook.

Whether or not Paul subconsciously knew that he and Jane Asher wouldn't last, his music hints at a sense of conflict. The couple were starting to feel the pull of their separate lives, which would eventually pull them apart. Pure and lovely in its inspiration, "Things We Said Today" is a wise lesson in how perspective changes over time.

The song's hopeful story may not have been borne out by time, but it was still a favorite of Paul's. He told Barry Miles that he especially liked its chord changes and its perspective, saying, " . . . the song projects itself into the future and then is nostalgic about the moment we're living in now, which is quite a good trick." It was an especially good trick for a twenty-two-year-old songwriter who was used to living in the moment.

ON ANOTHER NOTE
Jane Asher inspired a number of Paul's songs during the five years they dated, but youth, diverging careers, and infidelity took their toll on the relationship. In a surprise twist, Jane ended things on live television, saying, "Perhaps we'll be childhood sweethearts and meet again and get married when we're about seventy."

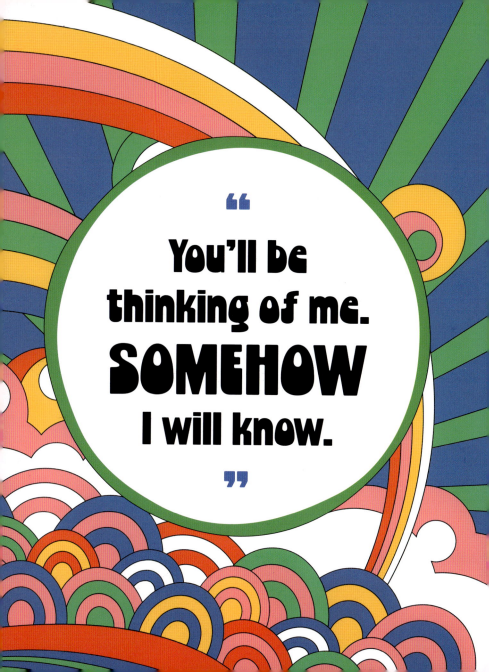

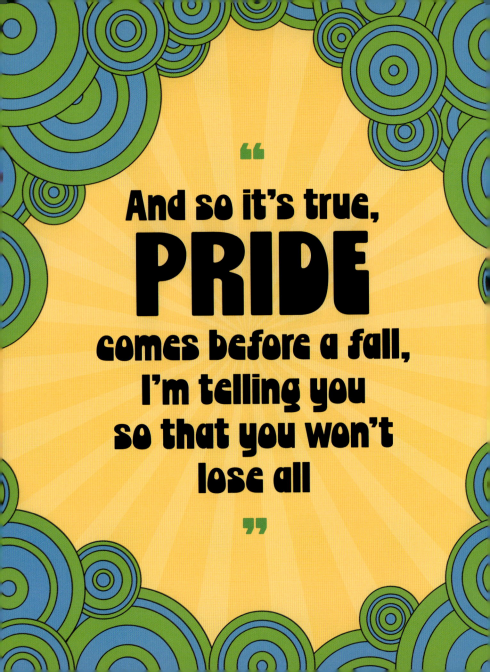

"I'm a Loser"
RECORDED IN 1964

No Beatles song is ever just one thing. With a rack-mounted harmonica, fingerpicking, and a bit of twang, "I'm a Loser" is intentionally part Bob Dylan and part country music. (John even attributed his use of the word "clown" to Dylan using it and, therefore, making it seem less "artsy-fartsy.") Combined with lyrics that offer their own emotional mashup, this hard-working song becomes far more than your usual breakup bop.

On its surface, "I'm a Loser" sounds like the story of a foolish young man taking his girlfriend for granted and losing her for it. But the song hints at something deeper. Paul believed that "something" was John's cry for help. He was presenting a happy face to the crowds while struggling internally with his own insecurity. Driving that theory home is how the lively tempo and uplifting harmonies contrast with the song's gloomy lyrics.

In 1980, John told journalist David Sheff, "Part of me suspects I'm a loser, and the other part of me thinks I'm God Almighty." For years, he dulled that disconnect with drugs, alcohol, and other self-destructive habits. He also used his music to work things out. In that same interview, John said, "I think everything that comes out of a song . . . shows something about yourself." Eventually, John was able to reconcile those two parts of himself. It's certainly no coincidence that a happy relationship followed.

> We need to learn to love ourselves first, in all our glory and our imperfections. If we cannot love ourselves, we cannot fully open to our ability to love others or our potential to create.
>
> —JOHN LENNON

"Yesterday"
RECORDED IN 1965

Born of a dream and written in solitude, "Yesterday" isn't your ordinary Beatles collaboration. In fact, the rest of the band felt they had no place on the track. Yet Paul's masterclass in elegant simplicity was an instant hit in the United States and remains one of the most recorded songs in music history.

Paul has called it "the most complete song I have ever written." Ever the counterweight to his friend and bandmate, John pointed out to one interviewer that the song is anything but complete—it doesn't resolve the narrator's sad predicament. But that's life. Too often, people are left to live with regret instead of resolution.

Although Paul wrote, "I said something wrong," the song brings to mind all the things left *unsaid* when you lose someone. Decades after recording "Yesterday," Paul admits that it may have been unconsciously inspired by losing his mother to cancer when he was just fourteen years old. The lyrics' sense of confusion and grief certainly support that theory, as does the regret so hauntingly put to music. But no matter the motivation, the lesson here is clear: Leave nothing important unsaid. You can't go back, and, for some, tomorrow may never come.

> **ON ANOTHER NOTE**
> Paul rolled out of bed one morning with the music for "Yesterday" fully formed in his head. At the time, he gave it the less-inspiring working title of "Scrambled Eggs." Because it came to him so easily, Paul was convinced he'd stolen it from someone else and refused to complete it for months.

"The Night Before"
RECORDED IN 1965

Love that fades may be harder to take than love that breaks. Without something concrete to point to, you're left to wonder what went wrong. "The Night Before" perfectly captures those feelings of confusion and hurt. But this song isn't some gloomy ballad, wallowing in what was. Instead, the Beatles infuse it with the energy of a chart-topping rock song.

Although the song's narrator begs the listener to go back in time, the Beatles only knew one direction: forward. At a 1965 press conference, Paul said, "We try to change every record. You know, we've tried to change from the first record we made." "The Night Before" continued that evolution with a quick tempo, bluesy guitar, and their first use of a Hohner Pianet.

The song wasn't a breakout hit, but it did find its way into the Beatles' 1965 movie, *Help!* The Fab Four filmed the scene on England's Salisbury Plain—the normally stoic location of Stonehenge—and seemed to be having a good time doing it. Whether you learn from the song or its creators, the lesson of "The Night Before" is a worthwhile one: Don't dwell on the past. Instead, start fresh in every moment.

> **ON ANOTHER NOTE**
> In his 1980 interview with David Sheff, John made his feelings about reminiscing clear, saying: "I don't have any romanticism about any part of my past. I think of it only inasmuch as it gave me pleasure or helped me grow psychologically. . . . I am only interested in what I am doing now."

"You've Got to Hide Your Love Away"

RECORDED IN 1965

The all-acoustic "You've Got to Hide Your Love Away" was, ironically, John's way of beginning to open up. He knew firsthand the difficulty of hiding his love—all of the Beatles did. Privacy was not an option in the spotlight. On top of that, manager Brian Epstein felt that female fans might be discouraged if they knew their favorite singers were spoken for. So, in the early days before Beatlemania, he instructed the boys to seem single even when they were attached.

John and Ringo both had to hide their marriages, forcing their pregnant wives to obscure their growing bellies in public. Years later, John would hide his affair with Yoko, too. He never hid his love of other artists' work, though. You can hear it in his songs—lyrics, riffs, and even instruments pay homage to his favorites. And it became his salvation.

John called "You've Got to Hide Your Love Away" his "Dylan period." He told David Sheff that hearing Bob Dylan's work inspired him to put more of himself into the song. "Instead of projecting myself into a situation, I would try to express what I felt about myself. . . ." John learned then that he could shine a light on all of the things he'd been bottling up and begin to create change.

> **ON ANOTHER NOTE**
> The Beatles inspired Bob Dylan right back, although he didn't often admit it in those days. He would later say, "They were doing things nobody was doing. Their chords were outrageous . . . and their harmonies made it all valid. . . . I knew they were pointing the direction where music had to go."

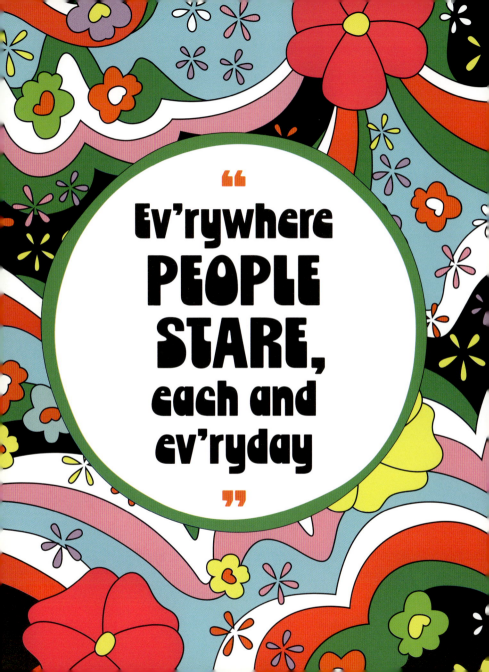

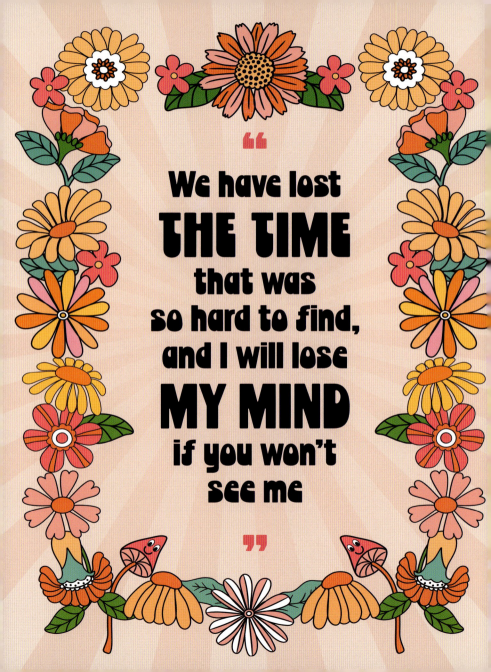

"You Won't See Me"

RECORDED IN 1965

Those moments when you have little time to think often give way to your truest feelings. In the rush to record three final songs in thirteen hours for *Rubber Soul*, Paul immortalized his. "You Won't See Me" is his bitter musical distillation of an ongoing disagreement with girlfriend Jane Asher.

Paul channeled into the song's lyrics his frustration with Jane prioritizing her career over his. The couple's independent successes often resulted in long separations and heated squabbles. Things came to a head in 1965, when Jane accepted a job with the Old Vic theater company in Bristol. The subsequent argument led to a short-lived breakup and Jane refusing to return Paul's calls.

A Motown influence on the music tempers Paul's biting lyrics. He took his inspiration from bass player James Jamerson of the Funk Brothers, saying, "It was him, me, and Brian Wilson who were doing melodic bass lines at that time, all from completely different angles, LA, Detroit, and London, all picking up on what each other did."

"You Won't See Me" wasn't the band's only tonal shift at the time. Paul would later say that the entire *Rubber Soul* album marked a change in the Beatles sound: "We had our cute period, and now it was time to expand." As they experienced greater highs and deeper lows, their music evolved. The Beatles learned that leaning into those experiences—good and bad—could only benefit them artistically.

> What I have to say is all in the music. If I want to say anything, I write a song.
> —PAUL MCCARTNEY

"Eleanor Rigby"
RECORDED IN 1966

"Eleanor Rigby" originally read "Ola Na Tungee / Blowing his mind in the dark / With a pipe full of clay" and featured a Father McCartney. But the moment Paul imagined the phrase "picks up the rice in a church where a wedding has been," he knew the true subject of his song: loneliness. And the song's characters meeting in death alongside the wail of strings masterfully captures it.

"Eleanor Rigby" came together quickly, with the help of George, Ringo, John, and John's childhood friend Pete Shotton. The group agreed on the name "McKenzie" (which they found in the phone book), Ringo added the line "darning his socks in the night," and Pete came up with the story's sad end. Paul and John took it from there.

The accompanying pair of string quartets were George Martin's addition, but Paul had terms for using them. He wanted the strings to sound "biting." Engineer Geoff Emerick obliged by placing separate microphones exceptionally close to each instrument, much to the musicians' discomfort. But the resulting song remains one of the most distinct in the Beatles catalog.

> **ON ANOTHER NOTE**
> The origin of the song's title character is a bit ambiguous. Paul has said he took her first name from an actress in *Help!* and the last name from a store in Bristol (Rigby & Evens Ltd). But years later, passersby noticed a headstone for Eleanor Rigby in the graveyard of St. Peter's Church in Woolton, which happens to be where Paul and John met in 1957. Upon learning of it, Paul said, "It was either complete coincidence or in my subconscious."

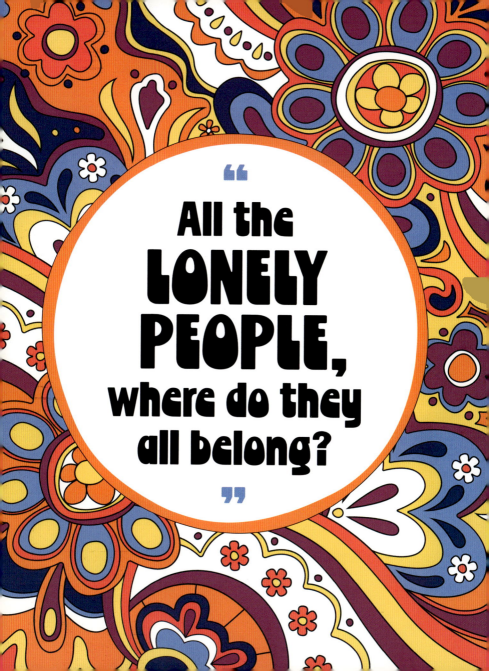

"She's Leaving Home"
RECORDED IN 1967

Although the Beatles had come to embrace telling their own stories through song, they had a knack for putting themselves in others' shoes. "She's Leaving Home" was a particularly deft adaptation of a story ripped from the February 27, 1967, issue of the London *Daily Mail*. The headline read, "A-Level Girl Dumps Car and Vanishes."

In the late 1960s, young women like seventeen-year-old Melanie Coe leaving home for love and freedom wasn't an uncommon occurrence. But something about the article struck Paul, who immediately saw things from the romantic's perspective. As usual, John provided the contrast, adding the parents' despair to the chorus.

John told *Hit Parader* in 1972 that he didn't have to search for the words. They belonged to his Aunt Mimi, the woman who raised him. "'We sacrificed most of our lives, we gave her everything money could buy, never a thought for ourselves. . . .' Those were the things Mimi used to say," he explained. "It was easy to write." With that added perspective, the song is able to explore the family's grief from both sides: the girl who felt misunderstood enough to run and the parents she left heartbroken.

> **ON ANOTHER NOTE**
> The song's muse, Melanie Coe, had actually met the Beatles prior to making headlines. She was in rehearsals for a lip-synching competition when she ran into them backstage on the set of *Ready, Set, Go!* in 1963. When Melanie won her contest, Paul presented her with her prize of an autographed Beatles album. But neither knew the extent of the impact they had on each other until years later.

"Hey Jude"
RECORDED IN 1968

One of the greatest songs of all time according to *Rolling Stone*, "Hey Jude" began as a wish for the happiness of John's five-year-old son, Julian. But it wasn't John who wrote the song that would spend nine weeks in the No. 1 spot (the longest of any Beatles song). It was Paul, who worried about how little Julian was taking his parents' divorce. The first pieces of the song came to him on the drive over to see the little boy and his mom, Cynthia Lennon.

Paul wanted to reassure Julian that better days were ahead. The song begins softly, almost like a lullaby, with just Paul and his piano speaking directly to Julian. Then the harmonies come in and the music builds as the thirty-six-piece orchestra begins to play, sing, and clap. With that, "Hey Jude" becomes a rousing anthem for those who have hit hard times, encouraging them to move through the pain rather than letting it weigh them down.

> **ON ANOTHER NOTE**
> John would go on to perform the song for years without knowing his son inspired it. In fact, he assumed Paul wrote the song for him. Things had been rocky among the band members and, with Yoko by his side, John had one foot out the door. To him, the song was Paul's way of saying, "Go ahead, leave me." However you look at it, the story of "Hey Jude" is a lesson in being there for the people you love.

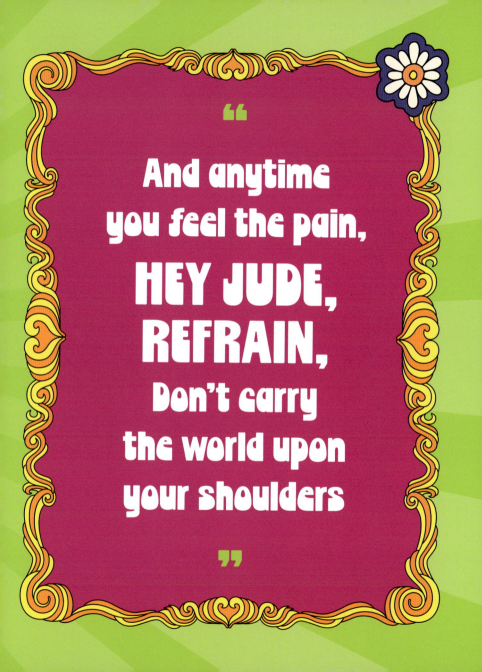

"Get Back"
RECORDED IN 1969

By late 1968, Paul could feel the band falling apart. In a last-ditch effort to revive the creativity, comradery, and collaboration that marked their early career, he proposed that the Fab Four get back to their rock-and-roll roots. But change had already started lapping heavily at their shores; the tide was about to come in and wash the Beatles away.

With the sound of "Get Back" decided, Paul and John turned to the newspaper headlines for the song's lyrics. Anti-immigrant sentiment was at an all-time high in Great Britain. An original line satirized the rampant racism, saying, "Don't dig no Pakistani taking all the people's jobs!" Fearing that listeners might interpret the line as sincere, they opted for the fictional stories of Jo Jo and Loretta instead.

But the song was just one part of Paul's plan to revitalize the band. The other was a behind-the-scenes documentary of the same name. Its finale was the band's last live concert, performed on the roof of their basement-level recording studio at Apple Corps. The performance captured the magic that had captivated the world for six years, but time and tide wait for no man—not even a Beatle.

> **ON ANOTHER NOTE**
> John told *Playboy*'s David Sheff that he felt Paul had a more personal motive in singing "Get Back": "When we were in the studio recording it, every time he sang the line 'Get back to where you once belonged,' he'd look at Yoko." Whether or not his suspicion was unfounded, it speaks to his mindset in those days before the band broke up.

"The Long and Winding Road"
RECORDED IN 1970

By late 1969, the writing was on the wall for the Fab Four. On top of the continual bickering and creative differences, John had announced that he was leaving. Paul channeled his grief into "The Long and Winding Road." He told Barry Miles, "It's a sad song because it's all about the unattainable; the door you never quite reach. This is the road that you never get to the end of."

Paul recorded a simple piano-led ballad that reflected his melancholy, but the song the Beatles released in 1970 bore little resemblance to his. Producer Phil Spector, hired by John to clean up a few of the tracks on *Let It Be*, had added an orchestra and a women's choir. Paul saw the melodramatic remix of his recording as a slap in the face, not just to him but also to the sound the Beatles had painstakingly developed over the past decade.

To Paul, "The Long and Winding Road" was the final nail in the Beatles' coffin. After the song was released, over his strong objections, he moved to dissolve the band. But every ending offers the opportunity for a new beginning, and this was Paul's. He announced his departure alongside his first solo album, *McCartney*.

> **ON ANOTHER NOTE**
> Paul credits Ray Charles with influencing the "The Long and Winding Road." The American singer later admitted he cried upon hearing the song for the first time. He released his own version of it in 1971.

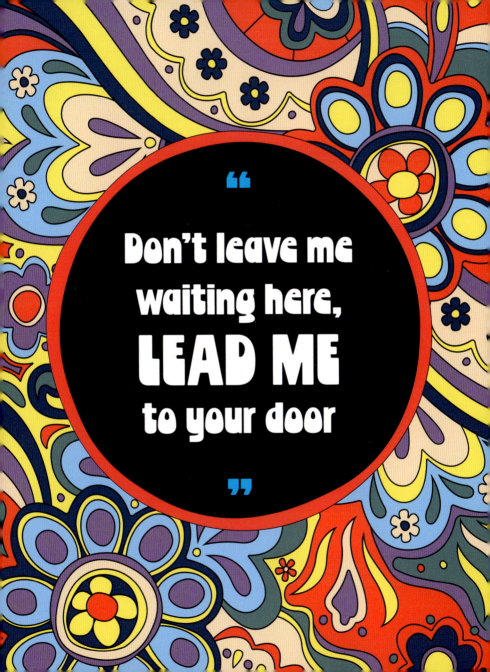

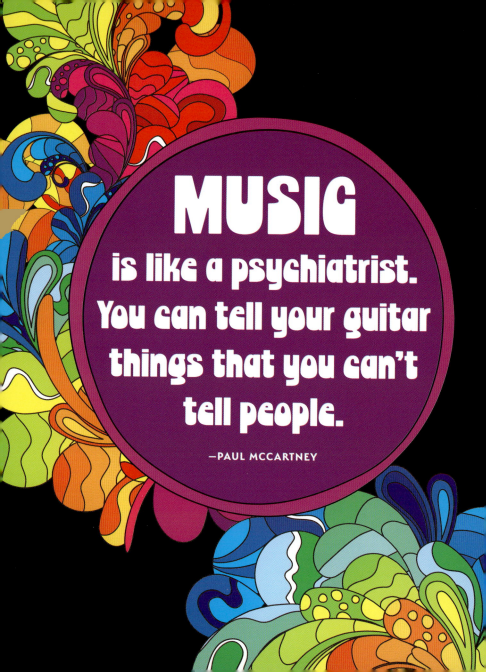

BETWEEN THE TWO TEENAGERS riffing on each other in their childhood homes and the four professionals recording in the studio, surrounded by industry legends, the Beatles had an extraordinary musical evolution. Through it all, they never stopped experimenting. They tried different sounds, wrote to diverse audiences, and did things to their instruments and recording equipment that exasperated studio executives. The Beatles' music has stood the test of time for many reasons, but their passion for it tops the list.

"I Saw Her Standing There" **92**
"Can't Buy Me Love" **95**
"I Should Have Known Better" **96**
"In My Life" **99**
"Eight Days a Week" **100**
"Day Tripper" **103**
"Paperback Writer" **104**
"Yellow Submarine" **107**
"A Day in the Life" **108**
"I Am the Walrus" **111**
"While My Guitar Gently Weeps" **112**
"Helter Skelter" **115**

"I Saw Her Standing There"
RECORDED IN 1963

The Beatles began to perfect their repertoire of chart-topping love songs in even their earliest days. But, as teenagers skipping school to write numbers like "I Saw Her Standing There," Paul and John weren't focused on romance. Their budding relationship as songwriting partners took precedence.

The duo hashed out the lyrics to what would become the first song on their first record in the living room of Paul's childhood home in Liverpool. According to Paul, John "screamed with laughter" at the first couplet, "She was just 17 / she'd never been a beauty queen." They ran through other possibilities one rhyme at a time until they agreed on the appealing ambiguity of "mean." The young Beatles finished their song with a base line stolen straight from Chuck Berry's "I'm Talking About You."

"I Saw Her Standing There" was what George Martin called a "potboiler," one of many written specifically in the hopes of garnering radio play. And the song certainly hit its mark opposite "I Want to Hold Your Hand" on the band's first single with EMI Records. That determination to write to their audience paid off, fortifying the Beatles' place in music history and allowing their talents to evolve naturally over time.

> **ON ANOTHER NOTE**
> The woman who inspired Paul's lyrics was dancer Iris Caldwell, whom he was dating at the time. Had Brian Epstein not talked him out of it, Paul would have given "I Saw Her Standing There" to Iris's brother. He happened to be Rory Storm of the Hurricanes—the band Ringo left for the Beatles in 1962.

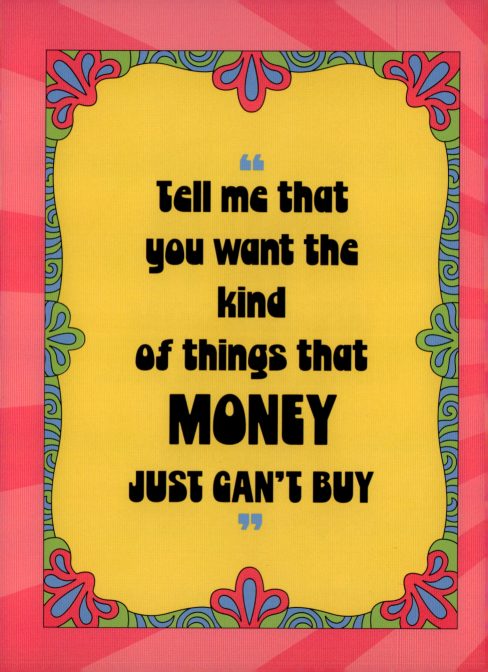

"Can't Buy Me Love"

RECORDED IN 1964

By early 1964, the Beatles dominated 60 percent of the American singles market. "Can't Buy Me Love," released at the peak of Beatlemania, proved no different, with preorders of 3 million copies in the US. Within weeks, it helped the Beatles set two records: They held the top five spots on *Billboard*'s pop singles chart and claimed fourteen of the Top 100 US singles. Decades later, they still hold both honors.

As much as they were leading the pack at the time, the Beatles were still primarily students of music. They looked to other artists and genres for inspiration, creating a sound that was somehow equal parts derivative and distinctive to the Beatles. For "Can't Buy Me Love," Paul wrote with the blues in mind, John added his rock-and-roll scream, and George used his solo to highlight his love of 1950s rockabilly music. But it was George Martin who thought to flip ordinary song structure on its head and start strong with the chorus.

That masterful collaboration and willingness to experiment are what catapulted the Beatles to international fame. (Although the mop tops and boyish charm certainly didn't hurt.) "Can't Buy Me Love" wasn't just another hit from this wildly popular foursome. It was the proof that this band had staying power.

> **ON ANOTHER NOTE**
> The boys recorded "Can't Buy Me Love" in Paris during an eighteen-day residency at the city's Olympia Theatre. They even had their room at the George V Hotel (near the Champs-Élysées) outfitted with a piano so they could work on their music, despite performing three high-energy shows per day.

"I Should Have Known Better"

RECORDED IN 1964

The relationships that make you reach for more and become a better version of yourself aren't always romantic. During their stay in Paris in January 1964, the Beatles discovered a new object of their musical affection: Bob Dylan. A French DJ gave the Fab Four a copy of his album *The Freewheelin' Bob Dylan*, and they were entranced. "For the rest of our three weeks in Paris, we didn't stop playing it," John later recalled. "We all went potty on Dylan."

"I Should Have Known Better" was the first Beatles song to feel the folk singer's significance. Although its narrator competes for a woman's affection, the song represents a different kind of push-and-pull. It marked the beginning of a career-long volley of influence and evolution between the music titans that changed the industry.

The folksy harmonica solo on "I Should Have Known Better" was just the beginning. Bob's impact on the Beatles—and especially John—became more apparent in thoughtful songs like "I'm a Loser" and "You've Got to Hide Your Love Away." And the respect was mutual. For the next decade, even after the Beatles broke up, Bob and John played off each other's titles, lyrics, and sound, advancing music with each successive song.

> **ON ANOTHER NOTE**
> The Beatles' history with drugs is well known today, but their first encounter with illegal substances is the stuff of music legend. Bob Dylan introduced the Beatles to marijuana the first time he met the band at Manhattan's Delmonico Hotel in 1964. According to Ringo, the evening was filled with laughter.

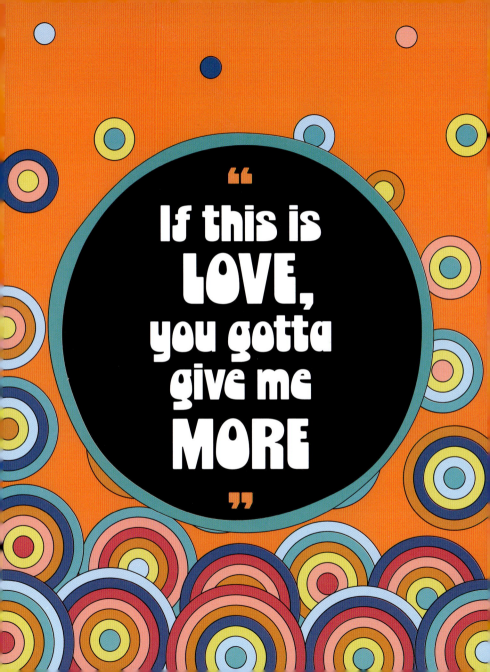

"In My Life"
RECORDED IN 1965

Despite the massive influence that the Beatles had on music to this point, John considered "In My Life" his first major work. It was the first song he wrote to express himself rather than to create a hit. He told *Rolling Stone* in 1970, "I had a sort of professional songwriter's attitude to writing pop songs. . . . I'd have a separate songwriting John Lennon who wrote songs for the meat market. I didn't consider them to have any depth at all."

That changed when journalist Kenneth Allsop asked John why he didn't write about his own life and experiences. Considering the question, John wrote a poem that traveled through all the places in Liverpool he felt influenced his life. But when he reread the poem later, he scrapped it. John told David Sheff, "It was the most boring sort of 'What I Did on My Holiday's Bus Trip' song, and it wasn't working at all." Then a new set of lyrics began to fill his head.

The resulting song, "In My Life," was a remarkable step in John's artistic evolution. It was the moment he began to trust himself and turn inward for his inspiration. In that moment, he learned that pouring himself into his music only made it better.

> **ON ANOTHER NOTE**
> Although the song is credited to Lennon–McCartney, how much of an influence Paul had on it remains a bit of a mystery. According to John, Paul wrote only the harmony and the middle eight. Paul, however, remembers writing the entire melody and adding his guitar riff.

"Eight Days a Week"

RECORDED IN 1964

Another upbeat love song with unromantic but fortuitous origins, "Eight Days a Week" added to a long line of hits for the Beatles. But the effort of producing the song proved that achieving success in the music industry was no easy feat. (The joyful young musicians only made it seem that way to ecstatic fans.) As George Martin said, "Success is a wonderful thing, but it is very, very tiring."

As with most Beatles songs, the inspiration for "Eight Days a Week" struck suddenly. Paul was on his way to John's when he asked his chauffeur if he'd been busy. The chauffeur replied that he was working eight days a week. Immediately, Paul sensed a song in the unusual phrase. But that song proved to be as hardworking as its muse. Although Paul remembers the song coming together quickly, John rightly called the song a struggle to write and record.

ON ANOTHER NOTE
Despite "Eight Days a Week" becoming a No. 1 single in the US, John told David Sheff that he thought the song was "lousy." The Beatles never played it live.

Between constant touring, writing, and recording, the Beatles were working eight days a week themselves. They were all but burnt out. But finishing *Beatles for Sale* in time for Christmas meant completing as many as seven tracks in a day. And this was the first time they had come into the studio with an unfinished song. Completing "Eight Days a Week" took fifteen takes, attempting a variety of arrangements over twelve days.

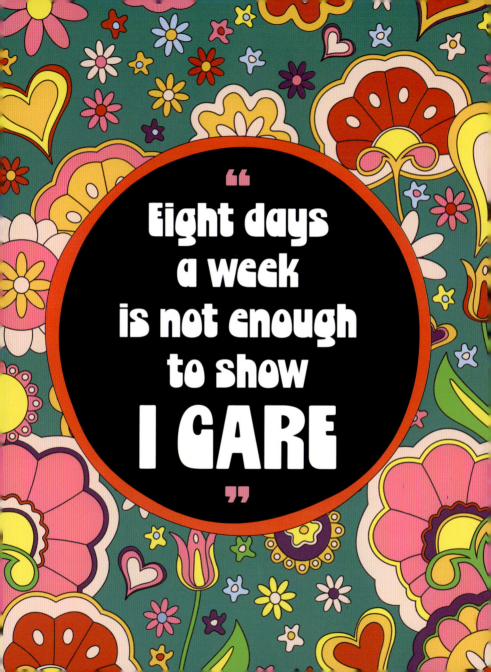

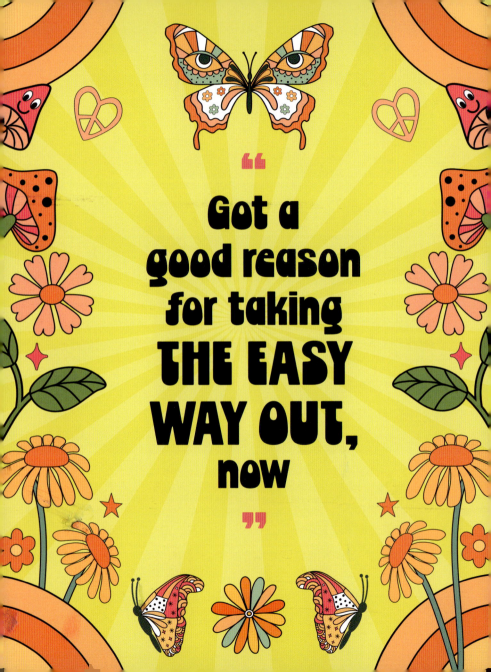

"Day Tripper"
RECORDED IN 1965

To fans, "Day Tripper" was little more than an up-tempo rock-and-roll song with a great guitar riff. But to the Beatles, it was equal parts cheeky fun and hard work under pressure. First and foremost, according to John, "it was a drug song."

Although they had smoked their first joint with Bob Dylan in 1964, it didn't take long for drugs to become a regular part of life for the Beatles. The heady combination of youth, unprecedented international success, increasing demand, and depression would be too much for most people. John told *Rolling Stone* in 1970, "I've always needed a drug to survive. The [other Beatles], too, but I always had more. I always took more pills and more of everything, 'cause I'm more crazy."

Rather than being reticent about their drug use, they claimed it proudly. "We saw ourselves as full-time trippers," Paul said, "fully committed drivers." "Day Tripper" was the band's way of poking fun at so-called "part-time hippies" so only their friends would understand. (The sexual innuendo in the second verse was another inside joke for friends.) Despite the mischievous lyrics, "Day Tripper" stands out in the Beatles' catalog for its complex arrangement and classic rock-and-roll flavor.

> **ON ANOTHER NOTE**
> John adapted "Day Tripper" from a folk song he'd written because the band needed a single on a tight deadline. When they recorded "We Can Work It Out" just a few days later, that was deemed the more marketable number. John adamantly opposed bumping "Day Tripper" to the B-side, so the band released the first "double A-side" single.

"Paperback Writer"

RECORDED IN 1966

One of the many reasons for the Beatles' fame and fandom was their zeal for pushing boundaries. From bringing in full orchestras in funny hats and incorporating rarely used instruments into their arrangements to writing songs with roots in every genre, they kept the music world on its toes. And their ingenuity was infectious, as evidenced by producer George Martin, manager Brian Epstein, and engineer Geoff Emerick pushing those boundaries right alongside them.

"Paperback Writer" started with an off-the-wall idea from Paul: to write an entire song in the form of a letter. He even signed the original draft "Ian Iachamoe," a pen name he used with friends that was based on the sound of his name played backward on tape. As much as fans wanted to pin his inspiration on a particular person, Paul later declared the song a work of fiction. That tracks with a 1966 interview, in which he said, ". . . I can tell you our songs are nearly all imagination—90 percent imagination."

Geoff took that originality and ran with it. In an attempt to achieve the richer bass heard on the Motown recordings made in America that the band envied, he removed the front skin of the bass drum and stuffed it with sweaters. He also placed a microphone just an inch away from it, in violation of EMI's equipment policies. (Venturing any closer than two feet could result in damage to the microphone.) EMI revised the policy when "Paperback Writer" soared to the top of all the charts.

> The Beatles saved the world from boredom.
> —GEORGE HARRISON

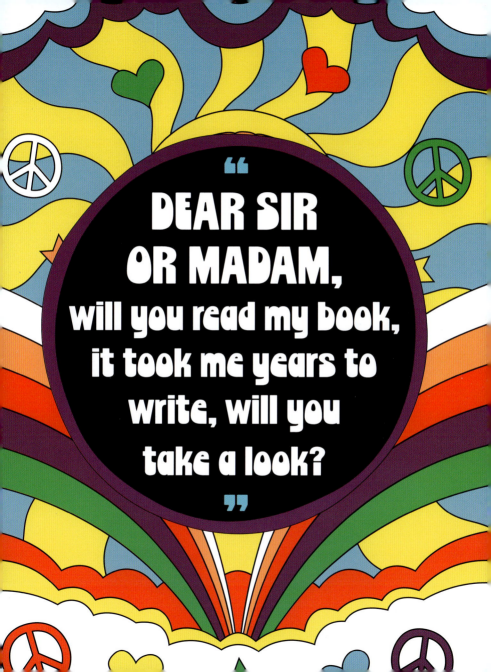

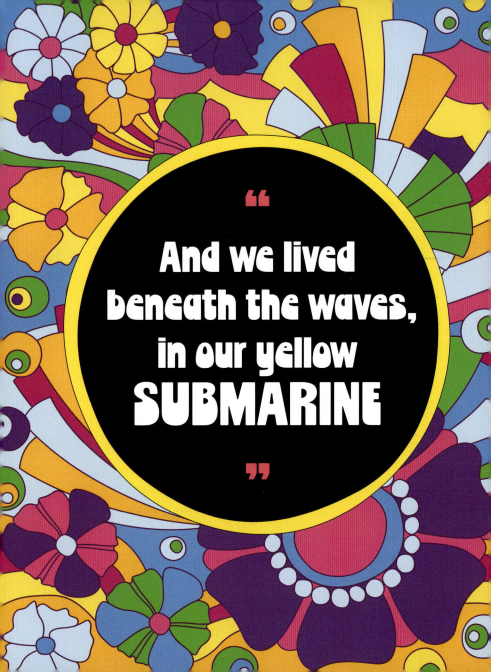

"Yellow Submarine"
RECORDED IN 1966

The Beatles' wide-ranging appeal is unlike anything seen before or since, especially considering their professional evolution. But that inclusion was intentional. While the band experimented with different styles and sounds, they also wrote with a variety of audiences in mind. And according to Paul, "Yellow Submarine" was first and foremost a children's song. He wrote it for Ringo, who had a way with kids.

Despite its innocent origin, "Yellow Submarine" was given the same raucous, drug-infused treatment as the band's other, more chaotic, hits. The Beatles invited friends and fellow musicians—including Brian Jones, Mick Jagger, Marianne Faithfull, and Pattie Boyd—to get high and help out with its recording. They grabbed whatever they could find to produce the song's sound effects.

The movie's creation was equally unruly. Brian Epstein thought it would be a great way to satisfy the band's contractual obligation to create another film. But, not being fans of *The Beatles* cartoon series, the Fab Four dragged their feet and indifferently threw together the requisite songs. In the end, though, they saw the movie's potential. In song and movie alike, "Yellow Submarine" has made Beatles fans of generations of young children.

> **ON ANOTHER NOTE**
> According to the 2011 George Harrison documentary, young Dhani Harrison grew up thinking of his father as a hippie who spent his days gardening. It wasn't until his classmates chased him around while singing "Yellow Submarine" that he discovered his dad's musical past. When he asked why he didn't know his own father was a Beatle, George nonchalantly responded, "Oh, sorry. Probably should have told you that."

"A Day in the Life"
RECORDED IN 1967

The world is a vast and varied place, full of order and chaos, beauty and horror, life and death. And the Beatles used their music to call attention to it all, carving out the remarkable in life's most ordinary moments. With "A Day in the Life," they turned those ordinary moments into a stunningly innovative piece of music.

John's inspiration for the song was simple: two randomly selected news articles in the January 7 edition of the *Daily Mail*. One was about the death of young aristocrat Tara Browne in a car crash, and the other detailed the finding of 4,000 potholes in the roads of Blackburn, Lancashire. When he came to Paul in search of a bridge, the pair combined two disparate sets of lyrics to create the principal work of *Sgt. Pepper*.

Recording "A Day in the Life" was nearly as frenzied as its orchestral accompaniment. Forty musicians each played their instrument from the lowest note to the highest while wearing party hats, rubber noses, and gorilla hands. To finish the song, John, Paul, Ringo, George Martin, and Mal Evans each struck the same chord on five different keyboards. Engineers duplicated and combined the sounds to create a goosebump-inducing cacophony.

> Reality leaves a lot to the imagination.
> —JOHN LENNON

Unfortunately, brilliant art doesn't always find its way into the mainstream. It didn't help that Paul's drug-inspired line, "I'd love to turn you on," caused the BBC to ban "A Day in the Life" from the radio. The song wouldn't become popular until after John's death.

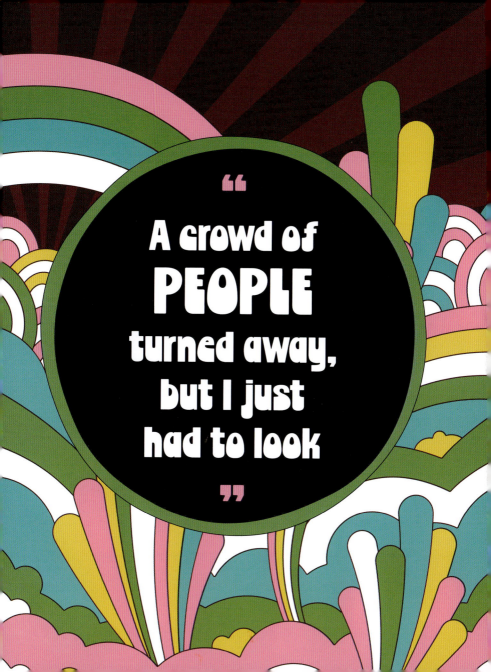

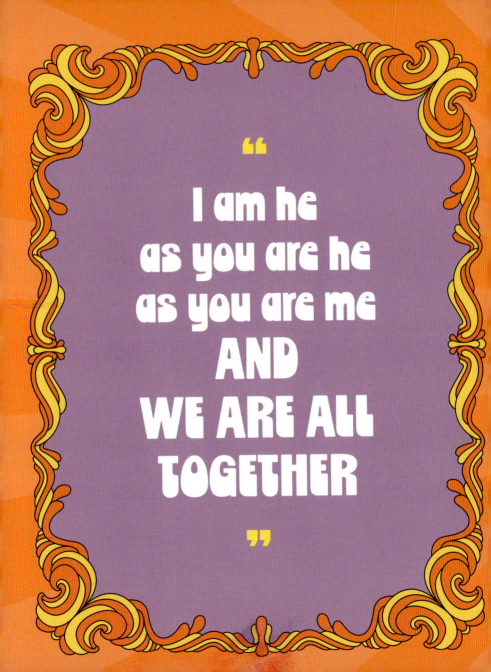

"I Am the Walrus"

RECORDED IN 1967

The sudden death of manager Brian Epstein in August 1967 left the band shaken, but Paul buoyed his friends by persuading them to work through their grief. That's when John came in with a song that befuddled everyone in the room. The powerful strangeness of "I Am the Walrus" was exactly what they needed.

Inspired by a local school that tasked its students with studying the Beatles' lyrics, John set out to write a song full of cryptic nods and nonsense. Appropriately, he chose lyrics and cadence in the style of Lewis Carroll's *Through the Looking-Glass and What Alice Found There*. Some lines were covert allusions—"Element'ry penguin" was John's way of thumbing his nose at the Hare Krishna movement—but most lines meant nothing at all.

In his 1980 *Playboy* interview, John admitted that filling the song with puzzling lyrics was an acid trip–inspired game, calling it the trick of "never saying what you mean but giving the impression of something. Where more or less can be read into it." But the song and its surprisingly complex recording gave fans plenty to talk about either way. Even in the face of their grief, the Beatles' music continued to walk the line between work and play.

> **ON ANOTHER NOTE**
> In 1969, fans began to take a darker look at the Beatles' albums. They heard words that weren't there, took clues from every photograph, and built an elaborate conspiracy: that Paul had died in 1966 and was replaced by a look-alike. The ambiguity of "I Am the Walrus" fed right into it, and some heard "I buried Paul" where John swore he said "cranberry sauce."

"While My Guitar Gently Weeps"

RECORDED IN 1968

Although writing and playing music came naturally to John and Paul, George had to work just a bit harder for every note. Perhaps that was why the so-called "quietest Beatle" had to fight to be taken seriously as a songwriter. Although "While My Guitar Gently Weeps" proved that he had the talent to compete with his bandmates, creating it remained a struggle.

By this point, tensions were high among the Beatles. (Ringo had just returned after quitting because of this.) George had an uphill battle getting any of his songs recorded, but he was especially disappointed with how cavalierly his colleagues treated "While My Guitar Gently Weeps." When its sessions proved discouraging, he turned to a friend for help.

While driving into London with Eric Clapton, George had a brilliant idea. He turned and said, "What are you doing today? Why don't you come to the studio and play on this song for me?" Eric was hesitant—he knew the others would balk at an outside musician playing on a Beatles album. But George insisted. Having the Cream guitarist in the studio seemed to help John and Paul focus, and the resulting recording stands as one of the Beatles' best.

> **ON ANOTHER NOTE**
> George found his inspiration for "While My Guitar Gently Weeps" in the *I Ching*. Eastern philosophy, he said, didn't believe in coincidence. With the idea of fate in mind, he decided he would take a book off his parent's shelves, flip to a random page, and write a song about the first words he encountered. Those words were "gently" and "weeps."

"Helter Skelter"
RECORDED IN 1968

"Helter Skelter" is yet another stunning example of the Beatles finding inspiration in their contemporaries. Intrigued by a critic's impassioned reaction to The Who's 1967 single "I Can See for Miles," Paul wished the Beatles could create that kind of unprocessed hard rock. But he drew a hard line between being inspired by someone else's sound and copying it. That line grew a little softer when Paul actually listened to the Who's song. It wasn't nearly as wild as he'd expected, giving him the opportunity to craft the sound he'd envisioned.

That sound was loud, raucous, and the complete opposite of the mawkish, sentimental ballads that critics had accused Paul of churning out. The band did a few takes, one of which lasted twenty-seven minutes and eleven seconds—the longest of any Beatles song. But when George Martin took an unplanned vacation, leaving the band in the hands of Chris Thomas, they let loose on the track. (According to technical engineer Brian Gibson, drugs were involved.) The band continued their unbridled cacophony the next day to finish one of the first hard-rock songs in history.

> **ON ANOTHER NOTE**
> Paul's song has held a dark association ever since police found "Helter Skelter" written in blood at the site of one of the Manson Family murders. But the title's namesake couldn't be more innocent. A Helter-Skelter is an English amusement ride with a spiraling slide. Paul used it as a metaphor for descending into chaos—an apt theme for the song.

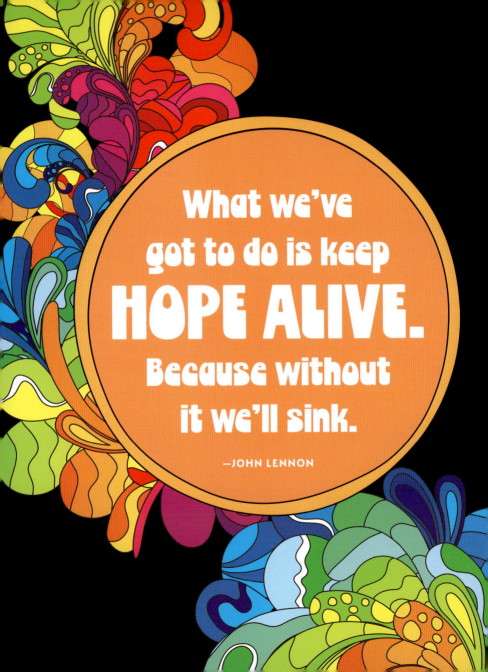

TALENT, PASSION, AND LUCK could only get a band so far—even a band like the Beatles. But hope kept them going. In the beginning, the four fresh-faced musicians dreamed of making it big. And when the band was running on fumes, it was Paul's characteristic optimism that kept them going. The Beatles infused their music with that hope from the first moment to the last, offering it up to fans as they were reaching for it themselves. Songs like "Good Day Sunshine," "Blackbird," "Here Comes the Sun," and "Let It Be" continue that legacy to this day.

"It Won't Be Long" **118**
"Help!" **121**
"Rain" **122**
"Good Day Sunshine" **125**
"Lucy in the Sky with Diamonds" **126**
"With a Little Help from My Friends" **129**
"Getting Better" **130**
"Blackbird" **133**
"Ob-La-Di, Ob-La-Da" **134**
"Something" **137**
"Here Comes the Sun" **138**
"I've Got a Feeling" **141**
"Let It Be" **142**

"It Won't Be Long"
RECORDED IN 1963

Another one of John and Paul's potboilers, "It Won't Be Long" offers the kind of double meaning that tickled the songwriters. While they sang about a person hoping for a reunion with their love, they were simply hoping for another hit. They mimicked the sound and style of previous ones, including the many "yeahs" of "She Loves You" and the play on words of "Please Please Me" ("It won't *be long* till I *belong* to you").

"It Won't Be Long" didn't have the commercial success that the Beatles were hoping for, but the song was an important stepping stone to the breakout hit "I Want to Hold Your Hand." And, although it was still early in their career, the song demonstrated how far the band had come in terms of composition and vocal harmonies in a short time. According to John's conversation with David Sheff, critics took notice. One remarked on the song's "Aeolian cadences," which brought in a more middle-class audience. In the interview, John retorted, "To this day, I don't have any idea what they are."

ON ANOTHER NOTE
While Paul later reminisced about how much he enjoyed playing with language for songs like this one, John was characteristically dissatisfied. He only recalled that he had tried to write another hit and missed the mark.

The Beatles soon discovered what we know today—that their biggest successes would come from innovation rather than imitation. And that innovation sprang from a deeper place of hope than "It Won't Be Long" did. It was rooted in their desire to make an impact through their music.

"Help!"
RECORDED IN 1965

Is it a straightforward rock-and-roll song? A complex composition with a reverse call and response? Or a lyrical confession that marked a dark period in one songwriter's evolution? As with so many of the Beatles' songs, "Help!" is a combination of all three things. Despite the band's tendency to quickly put together songs they said meant nothing, their music was never one-dimensional.

"Help!" was supposed to be just a simple title track for the band's second movie. But John admitted to David Sheff in 1980 that the song was his literal cry for help. He was depressed, overeating, self-medicating with drugs, stuck in an unhappy marriage, constrained by the band's newfound fame, and screaming to be set free. "Help!" became a turning point—in finally admitting to his own desperation, John made change possible.

With all that heavy emotion behind it, John understandably saw the song as a mid-tempo ballad. But he was persuaded to speed things up for the sake of commercial success. Despite achieving it and moving on to brighter days, John always wished he could rerecord the hit to be truer to its melancholy origins.

> **ON ANOTHER NOTE**
> Compared with the process of making *A Hard Day's Night*, the Beatles were upset with the lack of input they had on the movie *Help!* John later acknowledged that the director wasn't at fault for the snub. "We were smoking marijuana for breakfast," he said, adding, "nobody could communicate with us, because we were just all glazed eyes, giggling all the time."

"Rain"
RECORDED IN 1966

For a song that's just sixteen lines long and written about the public's invariably irritated response to the weather, "Rain" was transformational for the Beatles. It was the band's first intentionally psychedelic song, an attempt to capture the expansive nature of LSD. The lyrics offer a thoughtful optimism in telling audiences they have a choice in how they react to their circumstances.

The backward vocals in "Rain" were the result of a happy accident. In a post-work (and reportedly drug-fueled) stupor, John threaded a rough mix of the song the wrong way on his home recorder. He knew instantly that the disorienting result was exactly what the song needed. The band was so taken with the sound that they tried to apply the trick to their following album. Engineer Geoff Emerick later wrote, "From that point on, almost every overdub we did on *Revolver* had to be tried backwards as well as forwards."

ON ANOTHER NOTE
Ringo told Max Weinberg in 1984 that the drumming on "Rain" was his best work, saying, "'Rain' blows me away. It's out of left field. I know me, and I know my playing, and then there's 'Rain.'"

It wasn't just the backward vocals on "Rain" that helped set the tone for the album that followed it, *Revolver*. The song marked the beginning of a hallucinogen-heavy creative period for the band. As John put it, "*Rubber Soul* was the pot album, and *Revolver* was the acid." With "Rain," the Beatles stepped away from their pop roots and toward the next step in their evolution as artists.

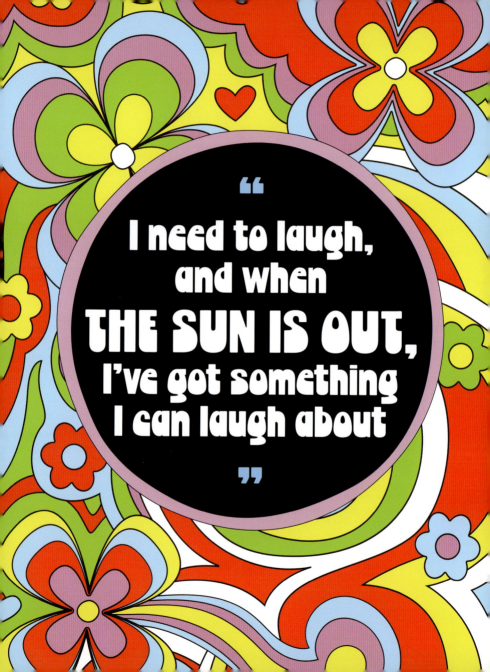
"I need to laugh, and when THE SUN IS OUT, I've got something I can laugh about"

"Good Day Sunshine"
RECORDED IN 1966

Inspired by the Lovin' Spoonful's mellow and thoroughly charming "Daydream," Paul set out to write a cheerful track in the same vein. "Good Day Sunshine" would end up balancing out the B-side of *Revolver* beautifully. Its optimistic lyrics are characteristic of Paul's personal philosophy and writing style, always the light to John's shadows. But it was producer George Martin who brought the energetic song to life.

By recording certain parts at different speeds and strategically layering them in, George created a more dynamic sound than the simple song alone could offer. He also volunteered his considerable keyboarding skills to fill in the middle eight, similarly slowing the tape recording to capture his solo. A section that would have sounded out of place at normal speed slips into Paul's piano chords seamlessly.

Paul later expressed admiration mixed with good-natured astonishment over the producer's innovations, saying, "George Martin [was] quite experimental for who he was, a grown-up." Despite the difference in age and background, the so-called fifth Beatle had a way of filling in the chaotic dreams of his charges. Few tracks celebrate his contribution as well as "Good Day Sunshine," a song infused with the hope and happiness of a band fully immersed in its heyday.

I've always been an optimistic person, because I don't like the alternative!
—PAUL MCCARTNEY

"Lucy in the Sky with Diamonds"

RECORDED IN 1967

Although many mistook "Lucy in the Sky with Diamonds" as another allusion to LSD (it was even banned for it by the BBC upon its release), the song has much sweeter origins. John's four-year-old son, Julian, brought home a drawing he did at school of his classmate Lucy O'Donnell surrounded by stars. He called it "Lucy in the Sky with Diamonds." When John shared with picture, Julian's doting uncle Paul agreed that it was perfect inspiration for a song.

ON ANOTHER NOTE
As a teenager, Lucy O'Donnell tried to tell friends that she was the Beatles' inspiration for "Lucy in the Sky with Diamonds." But they bought into the rumors of the song's ties to LSD. Afraid to admit that she didn't know what LSD was, Lucy didn't argue.

John channeled his childlike wonder and love of *Through the Looking-Glass* for the rest of the lyrics, envisioning a fantastical world befitting his son's creativity. In his interview with David Sheff, John explained, "It was Alice in the boat. She is buying an egg and it turns into Humpty-Dumpty. The woman serving in the shop turns into a sheep, and the next minute they are rowing in a rowing boat somewhere, and I was visualizing that."

Although it was Paul who added the girl with the kaleidoscope eyes, John immediately took to the description. In her, he saw a woman who could save him from the life and marriage he found increasingly miserable. In his 1980 interview with Sheff, John mused that the song foreshadowed Yoko's influence on his life.

"With a Little Help from My Friends"

RECORDED IN 1967

The hopeful message of "With a Little Help from my Friends" speaks for itself, but the Beatles also put it into practice while recording the track. Ringo was headed home for some well-deserved rest after an all-night session working on it. But his bandmates dragged him over to the microphone instead to sing lead vocals, standing around him for moral support.

Although Ringo was an incredibly talented and sought-after drummer, he wasn't as confident a singer as his bandmates. Still, he was a fan favorite, especially in the early days of Beatlemania—and the Beatles knew it. When the band played their famous set on *The Ed Sullivan Show*, comedian Mitzi McCall gestured to the screaming crowd and asked John, "Can you believe this is all for you?" John answered coolly, "It's not for me. It's for Ringo, actually."

George Martin made sure that Ringo sang one song on each album in the name of good marketing. Someone had decided that "With a Little Help from My Friends" was that song for *Sgt. Pepper*, and the other three Beatles decided that the time had come. With a little help from his friends, a wearied and nervous Ringo Starr sang the song masterfully.

> **ON ANOTHER NOTE**
> Paul later confessed that he and John giggled through their writing session at John's line, "What do you see when you turn out the light? I can't tell you, but I know it's mine." In their minds, it was just an off-color joke. But they knew fans would find a deeper meaning in it.

"Getting Better"
RECORDED IN 1967

It should come as no surprise that Paul came up with the idea for "Getting Better." While enjoying a walk on a lovely spring morning with his dog, Martha, and journalist Hunter Davies, Paul remarked, "It's getting better" (meaning the weather). Then he let out a laugh. Paul told Hunter that "It's getting better" was a phrase often used by substitute drummer Jimmie Nicol to describe having to deal with the chaos of Beatlemania.

When Paul began writing the song with John, the latter's characteristically acerbic response was "It couldn't get no worse." From there, the song became a perfect representation of the dichotomy between the two songwriters. While Paul lightly admonished his teachers, John wrote candidly about his cruelty toward women.

John admitted in his *Playboy* interview that he was physically abusive in his relationships. "I was a hitter," he said. "I couldn't express myself and I hit. I fought men and I hit women." His quest for peace, he said, was a result of his own regret and reformation. Just like the lyrics of "Getting Better," John himself came around to some of Paul's hopefulness in the end.

> **ON ANOTHER NOTE**
> During the recording of "Getting Better," John accidentally took acid when he meant to take an amphetamine. A well-meaning George Martin escorted the "sick" Beatle to the roof for fresh air. (The building's entrances were mobbed by fans.) When Paul and George Harrison realized what had happened, they raced to the roof to rescue John, who was quietly contemplating the universe under the stars.

"Blackbird"

RECORDED IN 1968

Writing during a time of great upheaval in the world, the Beatles often found inspiration in the injustices that surrounded them. They used their music to not only express their opinions but also to offer hope and support to those affected. Elegant and uplifting in its acoustic simplicity, "Blackbird" was Paul's way of doing just that. "This was really a song from me to a Black woman, experiencing these problems in the States," he said.

Paul kept the true meaning of the song veiled in symbolism so that anyone who heard it could find encouragement in its lyrics. The lesson "Blackbird" imparts is twofold: that you have the inner strength and resilience to overcome any challenge, and the power to help others through their own struggles.

"Blackbird" was a solo endeavor for Paul, who wrote the song at his farm in Scotland and recorded it by himself while his bandmates were working on other projects. After several attempts and additions, Paul decided that he wanted to keep things uncomplicated. He finished the final recording in the fresh air with only his voice, his guitar, and the beat of his own foot tapping.

> **ON ANOTHER NOTE**
> The first chords of "Blackbird" were inspired by a party trick of Paul and George's when they were growing up in Liverpool. They played a version of Bach's "Bourrée in E minor" to, as Paul put it, "show people that we were not quite as thick as we looked."

"Ob-La-Di, Ob-La-Da"
RECORDED IN 1968

The Beatles wrote many songs while surrounded by the meditative trappings of Rishikesh, but "Ob-La-Di, Ob-La-Da" certainly stands out among them. Its uplifting message is not far from the teachings of Maharishi Mahesh Yogi, who valued happiness above all else. But no one would call this song *peaceful* or *reflective*.

The unusual title and chorus came from a Yoruba phrase often repeated by Nigerian musician Jimmy Anonmuogharan Scott Emuakpor, or Jimmy Scott to friends on the London club circuit. When Paul heard it, he told Jimmy he knew he would use it in a song. (Jimmy was upset to not receive a songwriting credit for "Ob-La-Di, Ob-La-Da," but Paul gave credit where it was due and wrote him a check.)

Naturally, John disliked the simple, upbeat song and complained about the amount of time the band spent on it. He wasn't the only one. Everyone involved in the sessions was running out of patience with Paul's perfectionism. Tensions grew with every take—John stormed out, George Martin left after being berated by Paul, and Geoff Emerick swore never to record another Beatles album. The band was coming apart at the seams. Although "Ob-La-Di, Ob-La-Da" went on to become one of the most popular songs on *The Beatles* (a.k.a. the White Album), its hopeful message couldn't save the Beatles.

> **ON ANOTHER NOTE**
> George was befuddled by Paul's writing style. The former took a more personal, introspective approach, while the latter seemed to create something from nothing. Paul said that's exactly what he does—he creates characters that fans can relate to, just as a novelist would do.

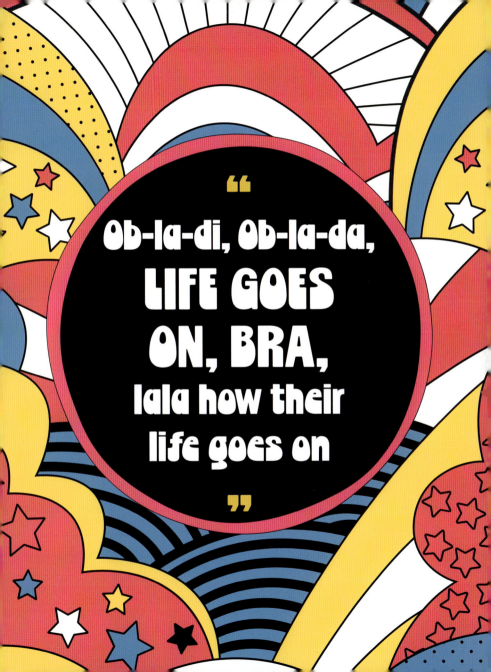

"Something"
RECORDED IN 1969

Hope doesn't come as easily to some as it does to others. After years of pushing himself, only to have his efforts belittled by John and Paul, George didn't allow himself to hope that "Something" was actually as good as he thought it was. It came too easily to him, he thought, so it must have been someone else's. When others assured him it was good, he still felt it wasn't good enough for the Beatles. He gave the song to Joe Cocker instead.

Engineer Glyn Johns remembered George asking him to stay late to work on "Something" so that no one else would hear it: "He was terribly nice, as if he was imposing on me. And then he plays this song that just completely blows me away." When the other Beatles heard it, they felt the same way. After months of work, during which time George took a turn at directing Paul for once, the song became his first A-side single.

> **ON ANOTHER NOTE**
> Originally, George thought he'd heard Ray Charles sing "Something," so he shelved it until he was sure it was his own. Ray would go on to cover the song in 1970.

"Something" proved that George had the potential to be as great as John and Paul, if only he'd had the support they did. By stepping out of his comfort zone, he created what Frank Sinatra himself described as "the greatest love song of the past fifty years." Today, "Something" is second only to "Yesterday" in the list of most covered Beatles songs.

"Here Comes the Sun"
RECORDED IN 1969

Shortly after stunning his bandmates with "Something," George delivered another wonderful surprise. Between the infighting and endless demands by accountants and attorneys, George had had enough. His decision to play hooky and let off steam inspired one of the most quintessential songs in Beatles history. "Here Comes the Sun" was a much-needed bit of cheer during an especially bleak time in the band's career.

On that fateful day off in 1969, George found himself relaxing in Eric Clapton's garden with one of Eric's acoustic guitars in hand. As the Cream guitarist recounts in his autobiography, it was a lovely spring morning. "We had our guitars and were just strumming away when he started singing 'de da de de, it's been a long cold lonely winter,'" he says, "and bit by bit he fleshed it out, until it was time for lunch."

> To be able to know how to get peace of mind, how to be happy, is something you don't just stumble across. You've got to search for it.
> —GEORGE HARRISON

When George returned with "Here Comes the Sun," Paul and John had to admit that he'd become a songwriting force in his own right. (True to the style of the two most competitive Beatles, that admission was both begrudging and understated.) Reflecting sometime later, Ringo said, "It's interesting that George was coming to the fore and we were just breaking up." But George's willingness to walk away from the darkness allowed him to find his own light.

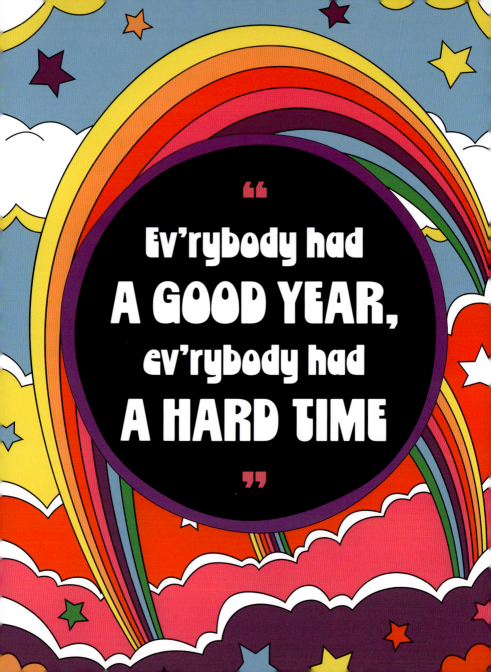

"I've Got a Feeling"
RECORDED IN 1969

Although many Beatles songs pit Paul's optimism against John's pessimism, only "I've Got a Feeling" merges two completely disparate unfinished songs into one. Paul's was a love song of the same name, while John's was a gloomy number called "Everyone's Had a Hard Year." Although their subjects couldn't be more different, their tempos matched. John and Paul decided to combine them.

At the time, Paul was newly married to Linda Eastman, and John was newly divorced from Cynthia Lennon. John was also feeling burned by the band not accepting Yoko and unhappy with being a Beatle in general. He'd also just been arrested for marijuana possession, and Yoko had just had a miscarriage. All in all, John had had a very hard year. But his tendency toward cynicism certainly didn't help matters.

You can see the struggle between Paul's lines and John's in the song's lyrics, perfectly encapsulating the songwriting partners' dynamic. Their constant duality shows us that hope is a choice, and a life-changing one at that. "I've Got a Feeling" was the last song the duo would write together.

> **ON ANOTHER NOTE**
> "I've Got a Feeling" was the third song that the Beatles played during their famous rooftop concert in 1969. The band hadn't yet nailed the song's recording, but the day's energy coupled with Billy Preston on electric piano proved just the thing. A recording of the live performance was used on *Let It Be*.

"Let It Be"

RECORDED IN 1969

Possibly the most reassuring song in the Beatles' collection, "Let It Be" came to Paul in a peaceful dream during a time of turmoil and tension. He saw his mother, Mary, who told her worried and weary son, "It'll be all right." It was a message that he and so many of his fans desperately needed to hear.

Paul told Barry Miles, "I'm not sure if she used the words 'Let it be' but that was the gist of her advice, it was, 'Don't worry too much, it will turn out okay.'" But Paul wasn't sure it would—his optimism was being worn down by the hostility he faced at work each day. Life as he knew it was about to change drastically, and, in the midst of it, he was losing a dear friend.

Paul had done his best to hold the band together, but he took his mother's words to heart. A month after the song's release, he released his first solo album and declared the Beatles broken up. Although an era of incredible music had ended, the musicians themselves were just getting started.

ON ANOTHER NOTE
John had effectively quit the band by the time the rest of the Beatles returned to the studio to do touch-ups on a few songs, including "Let It Be." The resulting single, which included a brass section added by George Martin, was released in early 1970. Meanwhile, John called in Phil Spector to produce the earlier recordings for the album. Paul thought Phil's mix was "terrible."

Sources

Beviglia, Jim. *Counting Down the Beatles*. Maryland: Roman & Littlefield, 2017. Google Books.

Chiu, David. "The Beatles in India: 16 Things You Didn't Know." Last modified February 14, 2021. https://www.rollingstone.com/feature/the-beatles-in-india-16-things-you-didnt-know-203601/

Cott, Jonathan. "John Lennon: The Last Interview." Last modified December 23, 2010. https://www.rollingstone.com/feature/john-lennon-the-last-interview-179443/

Lewisohn, Mark. *The Complete Beatles Recording Sessions*. London: The Hamlyn Publishing Group/EMI, 1988.

Margotin, Philippe; Guesdon, Jean-Michel. *All The Songs*. New York: Running Press, 2013. Kindle.

Miles, Barry. *Paul McCartney: Many Years from Now*. London: Secker & Warburg, 1997.

PaulMcCartney.com. "'You Gave Me the Answer'—Sgt. Pepper Special." Last modified May 24, 2017. https://www.paulmccartney.com/news/you-gave-me-the-answer-sgt-pepper-special

Rolling Stone. "100 Greatest Beatles Songs." Last modified April 10, 2020. https://www.rollingstone.com/music/music-lists/100-greatest-beatles-songs-154008/

Runtaugh, Jordan. "Beatles' 'Sgt. Pepper' at 50: John Lennon's Accidental 'Getting Better' Acid Trip." Last modified May 19, 2017. https://www.rollingstone.com/music/music-features/beatles-sgt-pepper-at-50-john-lennons-accidental-getting-better-acid-trip-122596/

Runtaugh, Jordan. "Beatles' 'Sgt. Pepper' at 50: Meet the Runaway Who Inspired 'She's Leaving Home.'" Last modified May 23, 2017. https://www.rollingstone.com/feature/beatles-sgt-pepper-at-50-meet-the-runaway-who-inspired-shes-leaving-home-124697/

Sheff, David. *The Playboy Interview with John Lennon & Yoko Ono: The Final Testament*. New York: Playboy Press, 1981 (Interview, September 1980).

The Beatles Anthology. Paris and San Francisco: Chronicle Books, 2000.